Order My *Steps*
VOLUME II

Walking in Confidence with God
A 6-week Bible Study and Journal for Women

Sheretta West

A publication of

and

Printed in the United States of America.

Library of Congress Cataloging-in-Publication Data

Order My Steps/West, Sheretta, ISBN 978-0-9961279-0-5

About the Study

As a young girl, I spent a great deal of my childhood with my grandmother. She was that busy missionary sister who was always on the go. If there was a need within our church or community, she did not hesitate to meet it. Her day usually consisted of making hospital visits to see sick church members, or cooking and delivering a hot meal to an ailing friend, or delivering groceries to a needed family. With all of her ministry responsibilities, she still managed to find the time to go fishing with her neighbor, Ms. Henderson. We were always on the move. It didn't matter to me where we were going. I just wanted to be on the move with my grandmother, watching her love and serve God's people.

Jesus disciples never had to ask him where they should go next. They knew to stay close to Him and simply follow where He was leading. While walking daily with God, you will not have to wonder if you are in God's will. When you walk in obedience and in confidence with Him, He will guide you step by step and take you to places you could never imagine. The disciples witnessed Jesus perform miracle after miracle. They experienced many sacred moments with Him. The joy of walking in confidence with God is the blessed encounters you will have with Him. The closer you walk with Him, the more of himself He graciously reveals to you.

You can enjoy this six-week study with a group or as a personal study. Pray before you begin each lesson. Ask the Holy Spirit to open your understanding to the scriptures. Each day you will go deeper into God's Word. You will meditate and journal prayers during the lessons. A good translation of the Bible is highly recommended. Consider using the New International Version. As you grow spiritually, consider going farther. You are encouraged to walk 10,000 steps each day. At the conclusion of each lesson record your total steps. Trust God to order the steps of your spiritual and physical life!

Sheretta West

TABLE OF CONTENTS

WEEK ONE

Bridle My Tongue

James 3:2-12

²*For we all stumble in many things. If anyone does not stumble in word, he is a perfect man, able also to bridle the whole body.* ³ *Indeed, we put bits in horses' mouths that they may obey us, and we turn their whole body.* ⁴ *Look also at ships: although they are so large and are driven by fierce winds, they are turned by a very small rudder wherever the pilot desires.* ⁵ *Even so the tongue is a little member and boasts great things. See how great a forest a little fire kindles!* ⁶ *And the tongue is a fire, a world of iniquity. The tongue is so set among our members that it defiles the whole body, and sets on fire the course of nature; and it is set on fire by hell.* ⁷ *For every kind of beast and bird, of reptile and creature of the sea, is tamed and has been tamed by mankind.* ⁸ *But no man can tame the tongue. It is an unruly evil, full of deadly poison.* ⁹ *With it we bless our God and Father, and with it we curse men, who have been made in the similitude of God.* ¹⁰ *Out of the same mouth proceed blessing and cursing. My brethren, these things ought not to be so.* ¹¹ *Does a spring send forth fresh water and bitter from the same opening?* ¹² *Can a fig tree, my brethren, bear olives, or a grapevine bear figs? Thus no spring yields both salt water and fresh.*

While walking with God this week you will learn:

• Though small in size, the tongue can do great damage.

• Never underestimate the power of your words.

• Stop complaining...start praying.

• THINK before you speak.

• It is possible to tame the tongue.

Song of Meditation: *I Surrender All*

DAY ONE

Just a Little Bit!

James 3:1-5

On a spring visit to see my son in the Bluegrass State, I had the pleasure of attending the Kentucky Derby. To see these equestrian beauties parade by with so much prestige, pride and even attitude was an experience to behold. While simultaneously displaying their style and agility, each race became more explosive than the last. Amazingly, their prancing, speed and intensity was not at their own discretion. Once the bit was in the horse's mouth, the rider could control the horse's entire body. It was the bit that made the horse obey. It pressed on the tongue, applying pressure to a sensitive area in the horse's mouth causing him to respond to the command. Without the bit, the horse was useless. What can you possibly do with an unbroken, unbridle or untrained horse? Under skillful hands, a bit makes it possible to break a horse, train him and control his whole body.

James paints a clear picture illustrating that the bit, rudder and a spark are very small in size with incredible power. Each is significant to control a horse, steer a ship or start a fire. These are all metaphorical pictures of how the tongue, such a little member of the body as a whole, can do so much damage. The tongue boasts great things and is very difficult to control (v5).

Read v.3-5. List three images that show the power of the tongue.

_____

_____

_____

Read the following verses that describe the tongue. Match each scripture with the correct corresponding statement.

1. _____ Psalm 52:2   A. deadly poison

2. _____ Psalm 64:3   B. sharpened razor

3. _____ Proverbs 10:20   C. a fire

4. _____ Proverbs 12:18   D. sword

5. _____ Proverbs 15:4   E. silver

6. _____ Jeremiah 9:8   F. deadly arrow

7. _____ James 3:6   G. healing

8. _____ James 3:8   H. tree of life

Correct Answers: 1.B 2.D 3.E 4.G 5.H 6.F 7.C 8.A

The tongue is described in many ways. Three descriptions (3) are admirable, and five (5) are harmful and damaging. Of the eight descriptions given, which best describes the tone of your conversations?

_____

_____

Is it possible to tame the tongue? What can a person do to keep from stumbling in words? How can we honor God in our public and private conversations?

My junior year in high school began to change in late March. In my driver's education class, I noticed that I had the eye of a young man. He was a tall, attractive, young preacher, a nice combo for a boyfriend. I hesitated to talk to him because of my little problem. I could curse like a sailor. No Judging! Without a doubt, I could have been an Emmy award winning writer for the HBO series, *The Sopranos*. I really did like this guy. I didn't want my potty mouth to discredit my Christian confession or my other good qualities. I shared my dilemma with my friends and they gladly offered to help me clean up my tart language. Their solution was to pinch me every time I would color my conversations with a curse word. Well, needless to say, many days I left school bruised and in pain. I cursed more because of the painful pinching. I shared my dirty mouth situation with an older and wiser friend. She said that pinching would not free me from cursing. The tongue is small, but it is a very powerful member and human endeavor would not tame it. This was a spiritual matter and deliverance would only come by the graceful hand of God. In a loving tone, she shared that my motive for wanting to correct this problem should be to honor God with my life and not to impress a young man. She also reminded me that I was a Youth Sunday School teacher and God required a higher standard of excellence and faithfulness from me. *Wow...that stung.* She prayed for me and encouraged me to ask God to help me represent Him in my conversations. God is faithful! Now I can use the same mouth to talk to my friends as well as teach a Bible study class.

Your conversations reflect the spiritual condition of your heart. Read Matthew 12:36. Discuss what is required of man on the Day of Judgment?

_____

_____

According to Matthew 12:37, by your own words what two things will occur?

_____

_____

Read Ephesians 4:29. What kind of communication is discouraged? What kind of communication does the verse encourage?

_____

_____

Your heart and the tongue work together. Meditate on Psalm 19:14. Journal your thoughts or prayers.

Secretariat, a thoroughbred racing legend could not have won the Triple Crown without a bit and bridle. You cannot go the distance with God unless He controls all of your life...even your tongue.

How has this lesson challenged your walk with God?

_____

_____

_____

What steps will you take today to go farther in your walk?

Physical Walk   _____

_____

Spiritual Walk   _____

_____

• •

DAY TWO
Lord, It's a Fire!

James 3:4-6a, Samuel 11:1-27

⁴ Look also at ships: although they are so large and are driven by fierce winds, they are turned by a very small rudder wherever the pilot desires. ⁵ Even so the tongue is a little member and boasts great things. See how great a forest a little fire kindles!

The tongue is a fire that has potential to do great destruction. It is a world of iniquity (v6), the seat of evil and moral unrighteousness. Because America is a country that upholds free speech, we get to experience the epitome of slander and mudslinging during the election seasons. I remember when Texas State Representative Sylvester Turner was leading in the election poles. He was a few days from being elected Houston's first Black mayor. One overzealous local investigative reporter broke a story that would raise questions about an alleged incident of insurance fraud. This allegation ignited a flame that would question Representative Turner's integrity and cause his support to drop in the election poles. As a result, these allegations cost him the mayoral election. Although a jury heard the evidence, vindicated him and found the story was false, the dye was cast and the damage was done. The spark of slander, character assassination, malicious gossip and false accusation can start an inferno that will stain a pristine reputation and destroy the lives of innocent people. Read the passage below and list the five potential disasters the tongue can cause.

"It only takes a spark, remember, to set off a forest fire. A careless or wrongly placed word out of your mouth can do that. By our speech we can ruin the world, turn harmony to chaos, throw mud on a reputation, send the whole world up in smoke and go up in smoke with it, smoke right from the pit of hell." (James 3:5-6 (MSG))

Have you ever said ungodly things to discredit the character of others? Do you lash out at others when things are not going your way? Do you curse the person that takes your parking space? Do you speak ill of the person who takes a longtime to order at the drive-through? Do you murmur against your supervisor? Never underestimate the power of your words. One of the first scripture verses that I learned in Sunday School was Genesis 1:1. My teacher, Mrs. Edith Roberson, made the creation story come alive. Through her soft-spoken voice, she would say, "Out of nothing, God spoke and worlds were created. God said, let there be light and there was light; God spoke and there was water, sky, land, vegetation, animals and man." God's words are powerful; they bring life, hope and purpose. We are God's children, created in His image. Our words have power as well. Life and death are in the power of the tongue (Proverbs 18:21).

As the world is full of sinful things, the tongue is a world of its own that is full of iniquity, wickedness, cursing, lying, gossiping, slander, anger, and wrath. Deep within each of us are degrees of iniquity: hatred, bitterness, jealousy, pride, and lust. Under the strategic orchestration of the enemy, the tongue takes hold of these and other destructive tendencies and actualizes ungodly behavior. King David was familiar with iniquity. He weaved a web of unrighteousness that was so massive it could cover a football field. Disobedience, abuse of power, deceit, lust, adultery, and the planned murder of a faithful soldier were a few of his offenses. Remember, the heart and the tongue work together. David ignited the spark when he began to lust for Bathsheba in his heart. The flames began to blaze when he said these life changing words to the messenger, "go and get her." II Samuel 11:4.

Read II Samuel 11:1-27 and follow David's web of iniquity.

_____

_____

The tongue is a world of iniquity and all kinds of evil that are in the world are presented there. David was close to God's heart (Psalm 17:8). He knew that he had sinned greatly against Him and was moved to conviction. With great remorse, he released his guilt and shame by crying out for God's mercy.

Read the following statements that express David's heart. Match the statement with the correct scripture.

1. _____	Psalm 25:11	A. I confess my iniquity; I am troubled by my sin.
2. _____	Psalm 38:18	B. Wash away all my iniquity and cleanse me from my sin.
3. _____	Psalm 51:2	C. Hide your face from my sins and blot out all my iniquity.
4. _____	Psalm 51:9	D. For the sake of your name, Lord, forgive my iniquity, though it is great.

The correct answers: 1.D 2.A 3.B 4.C

Though the tongue is a fire, a world of iniquity (v6). When what we do and what we say opposes the will of God, we can take note from the life of David. He repented and sought God's mercy and forgiveness. God is loving and full of mercy. He graciously forgives us when we acknowledge our wrong and our repentance is genuine.

How has this lesson challenged your walk with God?

_____

_____

_____

What steps will you take today to go farther in your walk?

Physical Walk   _____

_____

Spiritual Walk   _____

_____

• •

DAY THREE
The Source of the Problem

James 3:6b

And the tongue is a fire, a world of iniquity. The tongue is so set among our members that it defiles the whole body, and sets on fire the course of nature; and it is set on fire by hell.

James looks at the tongue from another angle. The tongue is not an isolated member of the body. It is that little spark that sets a blaze that defiles the whole body, ultimately destroying the entire course of a person's life. One afternoon we received an alarming call from my nephew, David Boyle Jr. A fire had mostly destroyed their home. He was awakened by the smell of smoke and, with presence of mind, he rushed his mother out to safety. They stood helplessly by and watched their home and much of their earthly possessions being devoured by ravishing flames. The investigation concluded that the fire started in the garage and the source of the problem was a faulty electrical system in the car.

Chaos and confusion don't just haphazardly surface in our lives. The words that we speak are often the primary source. Complaining, criticizing, threatening words, gossiping, judging or inappropriate conversations often ignite many marital and family disagreements, riots, political turmoil, social and racial injustices.

Read Numbers 12. Moses was a humble servant, God's elected leader. Why did Miriam and Aaron speak against Moses?

_____

_____

Read Numbers 12:6-8 and complete the following statements. God spoke to other prophets through the manner of:

1. _____ and 2. _____

Moses was a special leader with unique gifts and God spoke to Him:

_____

God was not pleased with Aaron and Miriam for speaking against His prophet. How did God respond to their insensitive complaining?

_____

_____

Miriam and Aaron's racial pride and prejudice, coupled with personal envy and public complaining, became dangerous to God's people. If their opinionated disposition went unpunished, it could have started a fire of protest and confusion among the Israelites. Their outspoken complaints were the result of jealousy and a desire for power. This was the source of the problem. God summoned them and brought their criticizing and complaining to a screeching halt! God will not sit idly by and allow us to speak ill of His people. There are consequences. Miriam took a 7 day vacation from the tribe. It was not a pleasure trip of comfort and relaxation. What she said caused her to suffer greatly: spiritually - the anger of the Lord burned against them (v9), physically - she was stricken with leprosy (v10), and socially - she was ostracized from the tribe (v14). Miriam's whole life was affected.

There are many lessons you can learn from this passage. First, Miriam could have spared herself much grief if she had only taken her complaints about the man of God to the God who chose him. Now, this will really make you think twice before you start to mouth-off about God's people. Miriam's healing was dependent on the prayers of Moses, the leader that she and Aaron foolishly criticized (v13). God will always have the last word! The person that you speak ill of may be the one you will need later in life: the employer who can hire you, the banker who can approve your loan, the judge who can dismiss your case, or the Spirit-filled women of God who can pray for your healing.

Meditate on Philippians 2:14-16 (NKJV): "Do all things without complaining and disputing, that you may become blameless and harmless, children of God without fault in the midst of a crooked and perverse generation, among whom you shine as lights in the world, holding fast the word of life, so that I may rejoice in the day of Christ that I have not run in vain or labored in vain."

How has this lesson challenged your walk with God?

_____

_____

_____

What steps will you take today to go farther in your walk?

Physical Walk _____

_____

Spiritual Walk _____

_____

• •

DAY FOUR

Spill the Tea!

James 3:7-8, Proverbs 16:28

⁷ For every kind of beast and bird, of reptile and creature of the sea, is tamed and has been tamed by mankind. ⁸ But no man can tame the tongue. It is an unruly evil, full of deadly poison.

²⁸ A perverse person stirs up conflict, and a gossip separates close friends.

At a Friday night Mosaic Women's Ministry event I was having a casual conversation with a young lady and I did the unthinkable. I broke the number one girl code, i.e. never ask another woman when her baby is due is unless you know for sure she is pregnant. I knew as the words were falling from my lips I had broken the cardinal rule. After I asked her that question, the silence was so thick. I live in Texas and could hear the snow fall in Canada. Suddenly, the sound of a big GULP broke the silence. It was me... swallowing my size 8 foot. The young lady responded in false humor. She flashed a big smile and said, "Aaah Mrs. West, I am not pregnant, I am just fat." Oh NO! I felt even worse. If I had only listened to the little voice in my head that was screaming...DON'T ASK HER THAT!

There are times when that little pink thing in our heads makes us say some regretful things. This week we have discussed the significance and the influence of the tongue. It is a small member of the body, but a destructive fire from the pit of hell that corrupts the whole life. Today, James looks from another angle at the disastrous capability of the tongue. It is unruly evil, disruptive, restless and out of control. It is Satan's instrument that is vigorously on the attack. Yes, the enemy will use any willing participant to slander, discuss or expose the secret and personal matters of others. Let's face it, we like it when someone spills the tea. Our flesh has an insatiable desire to hear the latest happenings in another person's life. What pleasure is there in disclosing privileged information about a person to those who have no business knowing it? Who benefits from gossiping about the faults, flaws and failures of others? How is God glorified when conversations maliciously reveal the secret concerns of others?

The book of Proverbs poetically describes the danger of gossiping and the hurt that it causes. Search the passages below. Write the damaging effects of gossiping.

Proverbs 11:13 _____

_____

Proverbs 16:28 _____

_____

Proverbs 18:8 _____

_____

Proverbs 20:19 _____

_____

Proverbs 26:20 _____

_____

Have you ever heard the phrase(s), "What's the dirt, the scoop, the dish or spill the tea?" Today on several talk shows and programs, gossiping is safely labeled "Hot Topics." There are people who actually thrive on discussing the faults and failures of others. They look for every opportunity to illuminate a person's shortcomings. For the record, women are certainly not the only ones who are guilty of repeating information shared in confidence. However, I Timothy 5:12-13 gives a vivid picture of a group of women whose reputations are somewhat disgraceful.

According to verse 13, how are these women described?

_____

_____

What three godly qualities would you want others to say about you?

_____

_____

Do you live your life in a way that will bring your desired response?

_____

_____

James said the tongue is unruly. Yesterday's lesson taught us the consequences of complaining and speaking against God's servant.   There are also consequences when our unruly tongue succumbs to the sin of gossip. According to the above passages in Proverbs, disclosing negative information about a person for self-gratification or sharing shameful details of others only stirs up troubles and causes confusion. Gossiping never builds up, it only tears down a person's life. It is a toxic recipe that produces anger and bitterness. In the book, *A Passion For Preaching,* Alan Redpath, gives a formula to apply before engaging in a conversation about any person that is possibly controversial. Before you fully engage, ask yourself,

T--Is it true?
H--Is it helpful?
I--Is it inspiring?
N--Is it necessary?
K--Is it kind?

If your response is non-affirming, then know that there are alternatives. You can sit in silence, change the subject or kindly excuse yourself. Those who guard their mouths and their tongues keep themselves from calamity (Proverbs 21:23).

Consider Alan's formula when you and your friends gather socially for an afternoon lunch or a Friday girl's night out. You can enjoy each other's company without discussing matters that betray a confidence or stir up dissension.

Meditate on II Timothy 2:16. Journal your thoughts or prayers.

How has this lesson challenged your walk with God?

_____

_____

_____

What steps will you take today to go farther in your walk?

Physical Walk   _____

_____

Spiritual Walk   _____

_____

· ·

DAY FIVE
Getting It Under Control

James 3:9-12

[9] With it we bless our God and Father, and with it we curse men, who have been made in the similitude of God. [10] Out of the same mouth proceed blessing and cursing. My brethren, these things ought not to be so. [11] Does a spring send forth fresh water and bitter from the same opening? [12] Can a fig tree, my brethren, bear olives, or a grapevine bear figs? Thus no spring yields both salt water and fresh.

The writer adds another description of the tongue; one that is as disgusting as it is ugly. It is full of poison that is as deadly as the venom of a snake. The Inland Taipan has the most toxic venom of any land snake in the world. It can kill an adult within 45 minutes. Conversely, the poisonous venom of an untamed tongue can literally destroy the life of a person in less time, literally seconds.

Why is it that man has the intellectual capability to tame almost everything else in creation- land, air and sea- but cannot tame the tongue? Is it possible to tame the tongue? It is amazing that a person can train their bodies into the perfect sculptured shape with six pack abs, buns of steel, and guns for biceps. The tongue is that member that you can't put on a treadmill or stair master to gain control to get fit. In the physical strength, the tongue is impossible to control.

In the early 70's, The Flip Wilson show was one of the more popular weekly variety shows. Flip Wilson would often play the character Geraldine Jones. Anytime she would do something that was offensive, buy a scathing outfit, or say something that was insulting, her immediate defense was "The devil made me do it!" Over time this became a national catchphrase.

Satan has no moral constraints. All evil comes from him. He is crafty and exceptionally skillful in any underhanded scheme. His ultimate goal is to destroy lives and he will use any available being to assist him in accomplishing his corrupt efforts.

Read John 8:44. According to this passage, how did Jesus describe the devil?

_____

_____

Satan convinced Adam and Eve that sacrificing their obedience to God would gain them everything. Instead their disobedience robbed them of all they had. Read John 10:10. Jesus said that the enemy has come for three reasons. List them:

_____

_____

The enemy is strategic in his attacks. He is not always obvious or ostentatious. According to I Peter 5:8, how does the enemy meticulously seek out his prey?

_____

_____

Each passage points to the destructiveness of the enemy. He wants you to speak lies, use profanity, destroy reputations, and kill character. When the enemy controls your tongue there is nothing good that flows for you. NOTHING! We are helpless in our human efforts. We don't have the strength, wherewithal, or mental capacity to handle this alone. It is a spiritual problem! The question at hand is, is it possible to tame the tongue? YES! Thankfully we have great hope and possibilities when we look to our Heavenly Father to take full control. God is the source of all good and righteousness. He is perfect. He is all-powerful and He alone can control our tongues. He is available to help us overcome every sin and evil that confronts His children. Surrendering our lives under His Lordship is how we can enjoy the benefit of this blessing. We give Him complete control and He graciously gives us the power of the Holy Spirit to help us.

Getting It Under Control – You are responsible for every word that you speak, tweet, text or post. Before you speak or push send, allow the Holy Spirit to filter your conversations. You can tame your tongue by:

1. *Daily committing your way to the Lord. Psalm 37:5-6*
2. *Surrendering your heart and tongue to God. Psalm 19:14*
3. *Relying solely on God's strength. Philippians 4:13*
4. *Speaking words that edify, encourage, and enrich. Ephesians 4:29*
5. *Asking for forgiveness for any ungodly communication. Ephesians 4:31–32*

How has this lesson challenged your walk with God?

_____

_____

_____

What steps will you take today to go farther in your walk?

Physical Walk   _____

_____

Spiritual Walk   _____

_____

Fire and swords are slow engines of destruction, compared to the tongue of a Gossip.

Richard Steele

WEEK TWO

An Exit Strategy

Genesis 13-14, 18-19

While walking with God this week you will learn:

• Trust God to help you make the right choice.

• God is a righteous judge.

• Bad company corrupts good character.

• Make sure your life is aligned with God's word.

• The past is behind you and a new life is ahead.

Song of Meditation: *Is Your All On The Altar*

· ·

DAY ONE

A Bad Choice

Genesis 13

Life often presents circumstances that require us to make major decisions.

How do I determine whether or not to discontinue life-support on a loved one?

Should I co-sign on a loan for my BFF?

Is he the right man to marry?

Is divorce the best option?

As a single person, can I commit to celibacy?

Is my 17-year-old daughter mature enough to drive alone?

Every day we are confronted with various opportunities to make decisions. Some decisions are as simple as deciding between cream or sugar; others can be the difference between life or death.

Lot was a righteous man who shared the tremendous faith of his uncle Abram.

The patriarch Abram was a wealthy man. He owned land and a large, growing number of livestock. Lot also acquired great wealth with flocks and herds. As their herds continued to grow, there was limited pastures and water available to maintain the livestock. Because the land could not support both, tension erupted between the herders of the two close relatives (v7).

Abram was a man of faith, prayer and peace. He loved his nephew and would not allow any quarreling to come between them. How did Abram propose to resolve this dilemma (v9)?

_____

_____

Have you ever had to make a major decision that would possibly affect your whole family? Lot had to decide where to relocate his family and flock. He could choose to go in either direction: north, south, east or west.

If you had to relocate your family, what are the primary necessities you look for in a potential location?

_____

_____

Where did Lot decide to move his family (v12) ?

_____

_____

Lot was drawn to the attraction of the lush and fertile Jordan Valley. He willingly moved his family near the city of Sodom (v10). It was a place saturated with wicked and evil men who sinned greatly against God (v12). The people were wealthy and enjoyed the exquisite luxuries of life and their behavior can be described as immoral, filled with selfishness and pride. They were promiscuous and perverted. This place was horrid. The people were morally insensitive to sin. Lot was a righteous and honorable man. Why would he relocate his family to a place that completely ignored the existence of God? How could they live faithful lives in a city that openly rebelled against God? This city was economically solvent so perhaps his decision was fueled by his ambition to amass more wealth.

My dear friend who loved God and lived a spirit-filled life much like Lot unfortunately found herself in a modern day Sodom and Gomorrah while at the workplace. She shared that she worked in a den of iniquity. She and her colleagues had very little in common, so beyond work projects, their conversations were sterile. She was not considered a team player because she refused to attend meetings in bars and clubs. The excessive drinking, flirting and foul language at interoffice and company gatherings were overwhelming. She leaped at the first opportunity to transfer to a new job. Shortly thereafter, the company closed.

Read the following passages; write the descriptions that each give of Sodom and Gomorrah.

Ezekiel 16:49-50 _____

_____

Zephaniah 2:9 _____

_____

Jude 1:7 _____

_____

List some challenges Lot and his family may have faced while living in Sodom:

_____

_____

We live in an ungodly world that bears all of the characteristics of Sodom. Can you identify with Lot? How do you ignore the temptations that this world offers?

_____

_____

Uncle Abram chose to lead his family near the great trees of Mamre, where he built an altar to God (v18). Abram had faith in God's promise to guide and bless him. His decision was not predicated on any ambition to gain economic prosperity. Abram's decision was spiritually motivated. His priority was to lead his family in the way of the Lord.

Lot did not see the spiritual danger he was putting his family in by choosing the fertile but corrupt area of Sodom. His decision did not bring glory and honor to God or yield favorable consequences. The Bible gives insight and principles to help you make godly decisions in life (Psalm 119:105). Read the following scriptures. Write each principle that will help you when you are faced with having to make a major decision.

Proverbs 3:5-8 _____

Proverbs 16:21 _____

Matthew 6:33 _____

Philippians 4:6 _____

James 1:5 _____

How has this lesson challenged your walk with God?

_____

_____

_____

What steps will you take today to go farther in your walk?

Physical Walk   _____

_____

Spiritual Walk   _____

_____

• •

DAY TWO
Guilty as Charged!

Genesis 18

While Lot was climbing the ladder of success and social status on the east side, uncle Abram was interceding to hold back God's wrath. Abram was sitting at the entrance of his tent and three messengers from God appeared. Abram was hospitable to these men but, before they left his home, they firmly informed him that Sodom was on God's hit list (Genesis 18:20-21). The judgment hand of God was on this wicked city and His wrath was soon to follow. The people of Sodom were past the point of no return. Repentance was far from their hearts. God gave the people of Sodom an opportunity to repent. They were so entangled in sin that they rejected His grace, lacked wisdom, and exhausted His patience.

God's judgment did not end with Sodom and Gomorrah.

Read the following passages. How did Jesus bring about judgment in each parable?

Matthew 25:1-13   _____

_____

Matthew 25:14-30   _____

_____

Luke 19:12-27   _____

_____

In Acts 2, the New Testament church experienced the miraculous move of God. Thousands of souls were added to the church along with persons being healed and other blessings.   Ananias and Sapphira had just witnessed God's graciousness to the church.

According to Acts 5:1-10, what ungodly act did Ananias and Sapphira commit that would warrant God's judgment?

_____

_____

Because they were dishonest, Ananias and Sapphira experienced divine judgment. What was their outcome?

_____

_____

How did the people respond when they heard what happened to the couple?   (Acts 5:11)

_____

_____

When God is judging others, this is not the time to sit idly by and watch in amazement. This is the perfect opportunity to examine your life and pray for His mercy.

Abram prayed for the salvation of Sodom. He was bold and persistent in his prayer. He asked God to spare Sodom if there were fifty righteous men. Well, there was not fifty, and not even ten. Abram did not have full knowledge of what Sodom had become, but he did know that God was merciful. Only God knows the full circumstances that provoked Him to unleash His wrath on Sodom and Gomorrah. God does not take any pleasure in destroying the wicked; however, He is just and He must punish sin (Romans 6:23) .

How has this lesson challenged your walk with God?

_____

_____

_____

What steps will you take today to go farther in your walk?

Physical Walk _____

_____

Spiritual Walk _____

_____

• •

DAY THREE
Association Brings Assimilation!
Genesis 19:1-10

¹ The two angels arrived at Sodom in the evening, and Lot was sitting in the gateway of the city. When he saw them, he got up to meet them and bowed down with his face to the ground. ² "My lords," he said, "please turn aside to your servant's house. You can wash your feet and spend the night and then go on your way early in the morning." "No," they answered, "we will spend the night in the square." ³ But he insisted so strongly that they did go with him and entered his house. He prepared a meal for them, baking bread without yeast, and they ate. ⁴ Before they had gone to bed, all the men from every part of the city of Sodom—both young and old—surrounded the house. ⁵ They called to Lot, "Where are the men who came to you tonight? Bring them out to us so that we can have sex with them." ⁶ Lot went outside to meet them and shut the door behind him ⁷ and said, "No, my friends. Don't do this wicked thing. ⁸ Look, I have two daughters who have never slept with a man. Let me bring them out to you, and you can do what you like with them. But don't do anything to these men, for they have come under the protection of my roof." ⁹ "Get out of our way," they replied. "This fellow came here as a foreigner, and now he wants to play the judge! We'll treat you worse than them." They kept bringing pressure on Lot and moved forward to break down the door. ¹⁰ But the men inside reached out and pulled Lot back into the house and shut the door.

While Lot was sitting at the city gates, hobnobbing with the rich and shameless, he was confronted by two angels. With humility and respect, Lot invited the strangers to his home and shared a meal with them. True hospitality comes from the heart. It's about opening your home and willingly sharing yourself and providing for the needs of others. It is sacrificial.

When my husband and I decided to buy a new home, I immediately began to pray. I asked God to bless us with a home where my family could be a blessing to our neighbors and friends. God is so faithful. Over the years, we have been blessed to entertain many of God's preachers and their families. Many of our friends stop by when they are passing through the city. Others, stay for a time to retreat from their ministry work.   Whether they visit for a day or a week, we were honored to have them in our home.

Read the following verses and fill in the blank.

Leviticus 19:33 - When a foreigner resides among you in your land, do not_____ them.

Proverbs 31:20 - She opens her arms to the _____and extends her hands to the_____.

Hebrews 13:2 - Do not forget to show hospitality to _____, for by so doing some people have shown hospitality to _____ without knowing it.

III John 1:8 - We ought therefore to show _____ to such people so that we may work_____ for the truth.

Showing hospitality is a beautiful gift of love that is almost obsolete in today's culture.   Abram and Lot both were hospitable to the messengers. During this time a person's reputation was largely connected to their hospitality.   Even strangers were expected to receive the same treatment as high honored guests. God's children are instructed to be devoted to one another in brotherly love and to honor one another above themselves (Romans 12:10).   It is not hard to extend kindness to others when you love God and live to please Him.

Both Lot and his uncle had unexpected visitors. What are the similarities and differences of the divine visitations? (Genesis 18:6-8; 19:1-5)

_____

_____

_____

Do you consider yourself as a hospitable person? If so, how do you show hospitality to God's people?

_____

_____

_____

Lot's hospitality came with a high price. His life took a sudden turn when he invited the messengers into his home. Before dark fell, news about the visiting men had gone viral and his special guests had become prey. The creeps really do come out at night. Every perverted man in Sodom convened at Lot's front door, vigorously looking for the two visitors. It is in v5-8 that you can see the perversion of the men, the ugliness of sin and why God was going to destroy this polluted place.

There is nothing glamorous about sin. It is ugly and displeases God. The Sodomites were shameless and flaunted their sin.

Write Romans 6:23 then memorize it.

_____

_____

In my lifetime, I have thrown a few people under the bus. And yes, I have a few tire tracks to prove that I have been tossed under the wheels as well. What Lot did to his daughters was absolutely unthinkable. He didn't throw them under the bus, he offered them to the wolves...and that's worse.

Read v8. What did Lot offer the men at his door in exchange for the protection of his houseguests?

_____

_____

Women were not highly esteemed then, but how could any decent father sacrifice his virgin daughters to a mad group of deranged men? Perhaps he thought since the mob desired men they would reject his daughters and leave. Not so! Lot wanted to protect his guests, but his suggestion gave a clear indication of how much of Sodom had gotten into him. Did he really think he could wear white and play in the mud? He sat in the square and had conversations and meals with them. He conducted business with them. He tried to reason with them and he referred to them as my friends (v7). He was painfully unaware of how much their lives had become intertwined and entangled. Yes, bad company will corrupt good character.

According to II Corinthians 6:14-15, God's children are instructed not to yoke together with unbelievers. This passage poses four (4) questions. Read below and give your honest response.

1. For what do righteousness and wickedness have in common?

2. Or what fellowship can light have with darkness?

_____

3. What harmony is there between Christ and Belial (Satan)?

_____

4. Or what does a believer have in common with an unbeliever?

_____

Has the light of Lot's influence and prominence diminished? Where you live, work, shop or get recreation are places that present opportunities for you to witness to the lost and shine the light of God's love. Lot compromised his walk with God. He was no longer a credible voice that God could use.

Do your family, friends and associates see you as a credible witness for God?

_____

_____

Or do you adjust your position and blend in with everyone else?

_____

_____

Consider the places where you traverse, are you living your life so that the indwelling Spirit of God influences others?

_____

_____

God's children are a chosen people whom He has assigned to lead those in darkness to the light of salvation.

Read I Peter 2: 9-12. Journal your prayer.

Lot lived in sinful Sodom long enough to have grown content with the ungodly people and their sinful ways. None of their wickedness seemed to faze him anymore. Instead of making an impression on their lives, he allowed their environment to alter his life. He had assimilated into their cultural patterns. Jesus had associates who were suspect: the woman at the well, Zacchaeus, and even Peter just to name a few. However, His relationship with them was solely for their spiritual security and not for any personal gain. He changed their lives.

Our position as God's children is to stand firm on our convictions and walk confidently with Him. We must not conform to the patterns of this world. Instead, our lives should always reflect the light of God, shining like a light on a lamp stand.

How has this lesson challenged your walk with God?

_____

_____

_____

What steps will you take today to go farther in your walk?

Physical Walk _____

_____

Spiritual Walk _____

_____

• •

DAY FOUR
Run For Your Life!
Genesis 19:11-17

[11] Then they struck the men who were at the door of the house, young and old, with blindness so that they could not find the door. [12] The two men said to Lot, "Do you have anyone else here—sons-in-law, sons or daughters, or anyone else in the city who belongs to you? Get them out of here, [13] because we are going to destroy this place. The outcry to the Lord against its people is so great that he has sent us to destroy it." [14] So Lot went out and spoke to his sons-in-law, who were pledged to marry his daughters. He said, "Hurry and get out of this place, because the Lord is about to destroy the city!" But his sons-in-law thought he was joking. [15] With the coming of dawn, the angels urged Lot, saying, "Hurry! Take your wife and your two daughters who are here, or you will be swept away when the city is punished." [16] When he hesitated, the men grasped his hand and the hands of his wife and of his two daughters and led them safely out of the city, for the Lord was merciful to them. [17] As soon as they had brought them out, one of them said, "Flee for your lives! Don't look back, and don't stop anywhere in the plain! Flee to the mountains or you will be swept away!"

Lot, the godly and righteous man that we met in chapter 13 has lost his influence. Read Genesis 19:9. "Get out of our way," they replied. "This fellow came here as a foreigner, and now he wants to play the judge! We'll treat you worse than them. They kept bringing pressure on Lot and moved forward to break down the door." The mobs of men were persistent and did not care about Lot or his family. Can you believe how boldly flagrant they were? They disregarded his status and his position at the gate. I'm sure the impudent men shocked Lot. They knocked on his door with a purpose that was obviously driven by their passion and lustful desires. If wickedness could be measured on a scale, this was certainly at the highest point. These men were unashamed and belligerent. That is what sin does; it gives a false sense of courage that lacks self-worth or respect for others. Lot's life was in danger. It is very clear they were trying to bulldoze over him like a pack of mad dogs in heat. The angels, the messengers of God pulled him back into the house. Deliverance! Yes, the angels of God saved his life. Lot had trouble on the outside and deliverance on the inside. Think about the time in your life when uninvited trouble came knocking at your door and God graciously placed godly people in your path to pray with you, read scriptures to you, sent angels to deliver you.

Pause now and journal your prayer of gratitude for the people of faith God has placed in your life.

Although the angels were on divine assignment they were also a grace gift to Lot. Their purpose for visiting Lot was not for a social gathering. It was two-fold. First, they had to extend a hand of mercy for the preservation and deliverance of Lot and his family. Next, they had to execute God's wrath of destruction on the city of Sodom.

Read verse 14. How did Lot's sons–in–law respond to his urgent request?

_____

_____

Lot finally decided to take a stand, but it was too late. Here again his credibility is mocked. His urgent cry that the Lord is about to destroy the city is equivalent to screaming FIRE!!! Unfortunately, his sons-in-law don't take him seriously. They could not receive spiritual truth from Lot because his faith was corroded and he had no spiritual power. This was a clear case of the blind leading the blind. It's one thing to warn a person about the coming of danger and destruction and another thing if they choose to reject the message. In this case, the situation is much worse. Instead of running for their lives, they laughed at Lot. They thought he was joking! They received a stern warning that destruction was at hand. Because the integrity of the messenger was questionable, the message was considered a joke, a moment of humor.

Can you honestly say that your Christian walk is aligned with your Christian talk?

_____

_____

In a relaxed atmosphere with your friends, can they sense your spiritual conviction?

_____

_____

Does your family or friends sense the urgency when you talk about escaping the wrath of God?

_____

_____

Has God ever warned you regarding a particular area of your life and you chose to ignore the warning? If so, which area?

Spiritual Life _____   Family _____   Relationship _____   Finances _____   Employment _____

God often gives His children warnings to prepare you for a situation or to help you to avoid one. He warns in many ways. Some are as subtle as a red flag; others are as ostentatious as a marching band. Walking closely with God opens your heart to hear from Him. Reading of His word, fasting, and praying to keep your heart sensitive to His directions is a daily goal. God's warnings are for your good, your deliverance, and your spiritual preservation. There is no need to speculate when He speaks, just take heed and run in the direction of safety.

Did Lot think he was exempt from the warning he gave his sons-in-law? Things are starting to turn up in Sodom and it appears he hasn't grasped the brevity of what is about to occur. The angels knew the exact time God would unleash His wrath. They firmly urged Lot to take his wife and daughters and get out of this godforsaken place. Again, Lot did the unthinkable. He hesitated...he paused! The city of Sodom is about to go up in flames. He should be running for his life. Why do you think Lot hesitated?

_____

_____

Lot willingly led his family into Sodom, but the angels had to drag all of them out! They took Lot, his wife and daughters by the hands and pulled them out of that perverted pit and told them to, "Run for your lives and don't look back" (v17). Use your vivid imagination and get a visual of the angels dragging this family to safety. That is the image of a person who procrastinates and has no sense of urgency about their spiritual life. Do you see how entrenched their lives were in this place? Lot fell into the materialistic sinkhole. He didn't want to abandon the lucrative, prestigious life that he had grown to love; the life of wealth, possession and status. Honestly...would you? His life was draped in the façade of success, money and power. We live in a materialistic world. Many people work all their lives to gain wealth. Their desire for money and possession exceeds their commitment to God or the things of God.

Read Matthew 6:24. "No one can serve two masters. Either you will hate the one and love the other, or you will be devoted to the one and despise the other. You cannot serve both God and money."

Have you fallen into the materialistic trap, desiring more and more things?

_____

_____

Give your honest heartfelt response, who is your master, God or money?

_____

_____

What occupies most of your thoughts, God or acquiring worldly things?

_____

_____

For the children of God, our first loyalty is to the eternal, the things that do not fade away. The things of this world are stamped "temporary." They can be stolen, worn out or taken away. Those who walk confidently with God have made the decision to live contently with Him.

How has this lesson challenged your walk with God?

_____

_____

_____

What steps will you take today to go farther in your walk?

Physical Walk   _____

_____

Spiritual Walk   _____

_____

• •

DAY FIVE

Eyes Straight Ahead!

Genesis 19:18-29

[18] But Lot said to them, "No, my lords, please! [19] Your servant has found favor in your eyes, and you have shown great kindness to me in sparing my life. But I can't flee to the mountains; this disaster will overtake me, and I'll die. [20] Look, here is a town near enough to run to, and it is small. Let me flee to it—it is very small, isn't it? Then my life will be spared." [21] He said to him, "Very well, I will grant this request too; I will not overthrow the town you speak of. [22] But flee there quickly, because I cannot do anything until you reach it." (That is why the town was called Zoar) [23] By the time Lot reached Zoar, the sun had risen over the land. [24] Then the Lord rained down burning sulfur on Sodom and Gomorrah—from the Lord out of the heavens. [25] Thus he overthrew those cities and the entire plain, destroying all those living in the cities—and also the vegetation in the land. [26] But Lot's wife looked back, and she became a pillar of salt. [27] Early the next morning Abraham got up and returned to the place where he had stood before the Lord. [28] He looked down toward Sodom and Gomorrah, toward all the land of the plain, and he saw dense smoke rising from the land, like smoke from a furnace. [29] So when God destroyed the cities of the plain, he remembered Abraham, and he brought Lot out of the catastrophe that overthrew the cities where Lot had lived.

God granted Lot enough time to make it to safety. God is patient. In His grace, He will hold back His wrath and give the lost an opportunity to repent and walk in righteousness and faith with Him. On the other hand, God's anger is also very evident toward those who are defiant and disobedient. Sin was at the core of these two cities. Again, sin will not go unpunished in the lives of those who continue to disobey. God opened up heaven and rained down burning sulfur; hell's fire on the twin cities.

Read v.23-24. In this story of Sodom and Gomorrah, what facets of God's character are revealed in these verses?

_____

_____

Against the angel's vehement instructions to not look back, Mrs. Lot turned back and looked at the smoldering city she once called home. She didn't just glance or take a quick peek. I used to run track in my middle school days. My track coach, Joyce Hall would always say, "Stay in your lane, run your race and don't look back until you have crossed the finished line." She looked back to the place that openly rejected God and she began to long for her old life there. Robert Plant says, "The past is a stepping stone, not a millstone." Her blatant disobedience to God's instructions cost her everything. She turned into a pillar of salt; a mournful stature that Jesus referenced as a warning to us in Luke 17:32.

Why was she clinging to a life God was trying to deliver her from?

Many years ago, I called myself a coffee drinker. Unlike most who enjoy the warm beverage, I would have a cup of flavored creamer with a spoon or two of coffee; sweet and hot. During the Lenten season, my sacrifice consisted of giving up all beverages except water. On Easter Sunday, I resumed drinking my cup of flavored creamer with added coffee. Well, that first cup was always a cup of poison. I knew what to expect because it happened every year: nausea, followed by excruciating headaches and just feeling horrible. I enjoyed drinking coffee and I only had to endure this self-inflecting suffering for about a week. About 15 years ago, after I had completed my 40-day Lenten journey, I decided I didn't want to go through a week of misery again. That year, I gave up coffee for good. On a more important note, my father died of diabetes and my mother is a diabetic. Yes, it is genetic. God showed me He was trying to deliver me from drinking five cups of pure sugar a day and move me toward a healthier lifestyle. Initially, I was too selfish and stubborn to see the grace gift that was before me. I have since learned when God sets you free of some sin, habit, circumstance or entangled situation, thank Him with a grateful heart, embrace the new journey and walk confidently in your freedom. If you must look back on your old life or habit, make sure it is solely to give thanks to God for where He has brought you.

Has God ever handed you deliverance and you rejected it?

_____

_____

Mrs. Lot had a new life waiting for her in Zoar. It was a place where she and the family could enjoy safety and escape the perversion and the wickedness of Sodom. It was an opportunity for a fresh start.

That is the gift of what God has for those who don't have a relationship with Him: forgiveness, healing, deliverance, restoration and a new life. Yes, a new life!

Everything that chained you to your past is taken away in Jesus Christ. As far as the east is from the west He removes our transgressions from us (Psalms 103:12). Praise God! He takes away the old life of sin, hurt, guilt, and shame and offers a new restored beginning with Him.

Are you that woman, looking back and longing for your sinful life while trying to move forward with God? You can't drive forward and in reverse at the same time. Impossible! Read the following passages and match each with the corresponding verse.

1. _____ Isaiah 43:18-19   A. To put off your old self... and to put on the new self.

2. _____ Philippians 3:13-14   B. If anyone is in Christ, the new creation has come. The old has gone, the new is here!

3. _____ II Corinthians 5:17   C. I have been crucified with Christ and I no longer live, but Christ lives in me.

4. _____ Galatians 2:20   D. Let us throw off everything that hinders and the sin that so easily entangles.

5. _____ Ephesians 4:22-24   E. Forget the former things; do not dwell on the past. See, I am doing a new thing!

6. _____ Hebrews 12:1-2   F. Forgetting what is behind and straining toward what is ahead.

Correct Answers: 1.E 2.F 3.B 4.C 5.A 6.D

When you accept the gift of Christ's salvation, your old way of life is completely in your past. You are no longer driven by the desires of your flesh. Walking with Christ you have a new role, you are no longer a slave to sin or the patterns of this world. You have a new stride, walking with a new purpose and headed in a new direction. So leave the past...in the past!

The question still remains, why did God preserve this family? Lot and his family were caught up in the Sodomite's shenanigans. Why were they allowed to leave under the protective hand of escorts? Lot's rescue was not because of any great moral quality that he possessed. We see how years of backsliding left him completely spiritually powerless. Now, let's be clear about why God preserved this family. He was granted favor because God remembered Abram (v29).

God has repeatedly shown His covenant hand throughout the scriptures. Read the following verses and fill in the blanks.

Creation is saved because God remembered _____ Genesis 8:1.

Israel is rescued from Egypt because God remembered _____ Exodus 2:24.

Lot and his family are saved because God remembered _____ Genesis 19:29.

Yes, uncle Abram was a man of faith and prayer. He knew God was going to destroy Sodom so he labored before God on behalf of his nephew (Genesis 18:16-33).

Abram prayed that God would save his family. God extended great mercy to Lot because of the fervent prayers of his uncle, a righteous man (James 5:16). I am grateful to have a mother who prays for me. I praise God for a grandmother who prayed for me. They prayed for my salvation and my journey of faith. God has placed people in my life that labor before Him on my behalf. Some I know and many I don't know.

Write the names of the warriors who pray for you. Pause now and thank God for them and the burden to labor in prayer for you.

_____

_____

How has this lesson challenged your walk with God?

_____

_____

What steps will you take today to go farther in your walk?

Physical Walk _____

_____

Spiritual Walk _____

_____

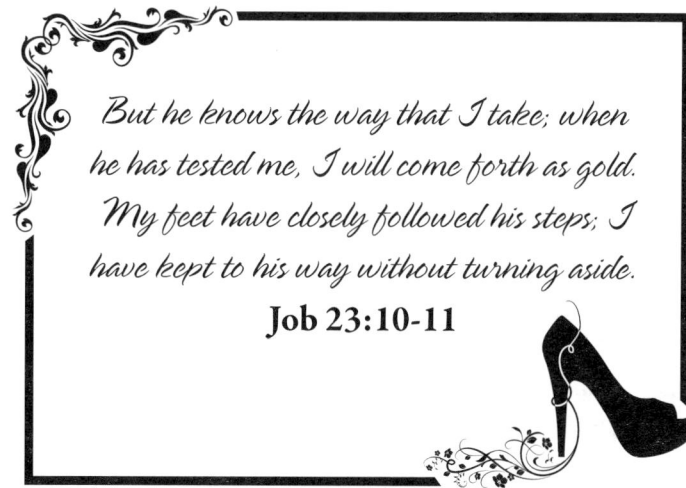

But he knows the way that I take; when he has tested me, I will come forth as gold. My feet have closely followed his steps; I have kept to his way without turning aside.

Job 23:10-11

WEEK THREE

Walking with Legends

The women of the Bible were real women and not fictional characters. Though our cultures are different, women today share many of the same challenges and concerns: marital, family, children, infertility, and many other matters that test our faith. When walking with legends, you can see God's ability to bring good out of difficult situations. Glean from the life of these legends. You will see what God has done and it will give you confidence in what He will do for you.

While walking with God this week you will learn:

• God will honor your faithfulness.

• The importance of becoming an instrument of God's will.

• Prayer expresses confidence in God's strength and power.

• Faith pleases God and opens the door to restoration and new beginnings.

• The blessing of walking with a legend.

Song of Meditation: *You'll Never Walk Alone*

DAY ONE

Abigail – Until Death Do Us Part

I Samuel 25

If you need a visual image of two incompatible people, then here you go: Nabal and Abigail. There are no details in this chapter about how they met or became a couple. I am inclined to believe this was definitely an arranged marriage or nuptials under some other involuntary distress.

Beyond Nabal's wealth and possessions, according to v.2-3, how do these passages describe:

Abigail: _____

Nabal: _____

Abigail was a special woman, beautiful in every way imaginable. Her physical attributes may have been slight in comparison to her character, intellect and wisdom. Her husband Nabal, on the other hand, was a piece of work. The Bible describes him as "surly and mean in his dealings" (v3).

The word "surly" is defined as: *unfriendly, hostile, rude, bad-tempered or arrogant.* Nabal was a wealthy and yet a miserable man. How awful that he is recorded in the scripture as such a Neanderthal of a man. His poor disposition certainly explains his rude response to David's request. David and his army of men were on the run from Saul. They retreated in Carmel where Nabal and Abigail lived (v2). David and his men kept a watchful eye on Nabal's flock. They made sure no harm or danger would come upon Nabal's shepherds or flock. Now, that's a good neighbor! David's added protection allowed Nabal's flocks to increase and Nabal amassed more wealth in the process.

One day, David sent ten young men to Nabal's home with warm greeting requesting compensation for David's act of protecting Nabal's sheep. Nabal grew another head and turned into a monster.

According to v. 9-11 what was Nabal's response to David's request?

_____

_____

It was one thing to refuse David's request, but Nabal twisted the knife when he went out of his way to humiliate and disgrace David. Nabal means fool (v25) and he certainly lived up to his name when he foolishly insulted the most powerful man in that region, the future King. Hear what Solomon has to say about fools in Proverbs, the book of wisdom. Read the following passages and fill in the blanks.

1. Proverbs 3:35 - The wise inherit _____, but fools get only _____.

2. Proverbs 10:14 - The wise store up _____, but the mouth of a fool invites _____.

3. Proverbs 10:21 - The lips of the righteous nourish_____, but fools die for lack of _____.

4. Proverbs 13:20 - _____with the wise and become wise, or a _____of fools suffers harm.

5. Proverbs 14:3 - A fool's mouth lashes out with _____, but the lips of the wise _____ them.

I think we can agree that Nabal was not a wise man, but his wife Abigail was a woman of wisdom. Once Nabal's servant informed her of her husband's foolish behavior, Abigail sprang into high gear (v18). She had to work fast because her household was in trouble. I am sure she was well aware of David's military accomplishments. She was also wise enough to know that David was a warrior and was not going to chew and swallow Nabal's insults. She was right! When David's men reported to him what Nabal said, he was FURIOUS!

What was Abigail's gift of appeasement (v.18)?

_____

_____

David's rage had him on a course that would affect his future. According to verses 21-22, how did David plan to respond to Nabal's taunting reply and rude behavior?

_____

_____

According to verses 23-31, this wise woman poured out her heart. What did Abigail do to avert David's plan of vengeance?

_____

_____

Read verses 32-35 and describe how David responded to her heartfelt appeal?

_____

_____

God used this woman of wisdom to not only secure her household, but to also leave a legacy of the future King of Israel (v30-31).

Abigail was wise not to share her plans with Nabal beforehand. After her meeting with David, she returned home to a drunken husband. When someone is inebriated that is not the time to discuss important matters. Timing is everything. Ask God for wisdom to know the best time for confrontation. Abigail waited until morning when he was sober and she told him what she had done. How did Nabal take the news?

_____

_____

After David heard of Nabal's cardiovascular demise, he praised God for keeping him from taking matters into his own hands. Abigail was married to a fool and gracefully fulfilled her matrimonial contract to Nabal; until death do us part.   He died and David immediately asked Abigail to be his wife. This time it was her choice to marry David...or not. She accepted his proposal and became his third wife.

Abigail made the best out of a very bad situation. She was courageous and a peacemaker. She stayed on the right path and God honored her faithfulness and generosity.

After reading Abigail's story, what other qualities do you see unfolding in her life?

_____

_____

What can you learn from Abigail when working or living with strong-willed men like Nabal and David?

_____

_____

How has this lesson challenged your walk with God?

_____

_____

_____

What steps will you take today to go farther in your walk?

Physical Walk   _____

_____

Spiritual Walk   _____

_____

• •

DAY TWO
Jochebed & Pharaoh's Daughter – One Son... Two Mothers

Exodus 1; 2:1-10

What would be your initial response if you saw a basket with a baby inside floating down a river? Pharaoh was afraid of the rapid growth of the nation of Israel. He felt they would organize as a nation and threaten the stability of his kingdom. To impede their growing population he enslaved them. He oppressed them hoping to kill their spirit. But the more they were oppressed, the more they multiplied and grew stronger (Exodus 1:12). Pharaoh gave the order that the midwives were to kill every male child that emerges from the womb. They chose to disregard Pharaoh's evil command because they feared God more than they feared Pharaoh. Their faith in God gave them courage to take a stand for what was right. Pharaoh's paranoia was at level red. When the midwives would not comply, he commanded his soldiers to search every house and throw all newborn males into the Nile River. Imagine the terror that came over every home that was blessed with a young son. Jochebed, the mother of Moses was a woman of wisdom and ingenuity. She could not comply with Pharaoh's brutal decree. She looked for ways to preserve the life of her son, so she hid her newborn baby for three months. Surely during this time she bonded with baby Moses. She resolved within her heart that if Pharaoh wanted her son in the Nile River, it would be by her own hands. How do you respond when you face evil?

_____

_____

Do you feel frustrated by how little you can do about it?

_____

_____

Ask God to show you ways you can act against any evil you may face. He will use your efforts to encourage others and to make a difference in your walk of faith.

After my sons would return to school from their summer or holiday breaks, our home would be so quiet. I would miss having late breakfasts with them, watching a late movie, or just laughing and talking around the family table. When they were home there was some level of comfort. On occasion, I would take a sudden trip and show up on their college campuses unannounced. Yes, I was that mom...no judging. They have matured into godly young seminarians, and they remain a prayer burden on my heart; praying for their continued safety and laboring for their physical and spiritual lives. I can't imagine the anxiety or rollercoaster of emotions Jochebed must have felt or the prayers that she prayed for her son.

Read Psalms 127:3-5. Journal a prayer for all children.
³ Children are a heritage from the Lord, offspring a reward from him. ⁴ Like arrows in the hands of a warrior are children born in one's youth. ⁵ Blessed is the man whose quiver is full of them. They will not be put to shame when they contend with their opponents in court.

What is your greatest fear for your children or the children of your family?

_____

_____

Surely, Jochebed pondered the uncertainties that were lurking ahead; Moses safety, his future, his destiny. Without a doubt this was an act of faith.

The moment she placed Moses in the Nile River, God began to navigate everything that followed. It was solely divine providence that synced all the participants. The under current, the strength of the wind, his sister Miriam, the slave girls and Pharaoh's daughter were all significant in creating a path that would change the course of history.

Moses floated down the Nile under the watchful eye of Miriam. She babysat her little brother from a safe distance.

Pharaoh's daughter decided to take a bath at the time the Baby Moses is floating down the river... coincidence or providence? She notices the basket in the reeds and instructs her slave girls to pull the basket from the water.

She opened the basket without knowing the significance of what was inside. When she sees a three-month old baby boy her heart was immediately filled with _____ (v6).

She recognized this was a Hebrew baby boy, a male child that was on her father's hit list. Moreover, she saw a child in need. Now she is at a crossroad and she had to make a decision. Would she follow her God-given motherly instincts and save this baby, or would she obey her ruthless father's command and empty the basket into the Nile? (Exodus 1:22)

_____

_____

Miriam was a courageous young girl. What did Miriam ask Pharaoh's daughter (v7)?

_____

_____

Did she accept or reject the young girl's offers (v8)?

_____

_____

What Hebrew woman did Miriam have in mind to fulfill this nursing mother's obligation (v9)?

_____

_____

Compare verses 9-10. What emotional challenges do you think Jochebed was facing?

_____

_____

Not only was Moses saved; he was also reunited with his family. The bonus was Jochebed was paid to nurse her own son (v9). Moses stayed with Jochebed until she weaned him from her breast.

On your walk with God, some unexpected opportunities may come your way. Don't allow doubt or fear of what might happen to cause you to miss a blessed opportunity. The midwives feared God more than Pharaoh and the Israelites continued to multiply. Jochebed acted in faith and her baby was saved. The compassionate heart of Pharaoh's daughter's overshadowed her father's brutal request. Miriam seized an opportunity and reunited her family. God used a slave and a princess to preserve the man whom He chose to deliver His people.

What unique qualities do you see in Jochebed?

_____

_____

What unique qualities do you see in Pharaoh's daughter?

_____

_____

How has this lesson challenged your walk with God?

_____

_____

_____

What steps will you take today to go farther in your walk?

Physical Walk   _____

_____

Spiritual Walk   _____

_____

DAY THREE
Hannah - Burdened...Broken...Blessed!

I Samuel 1

A few years ago, a dear friend shared with me how painful it is for her to attend church on Mother's Day. She said that all of the accolades and acknowledgements that are given to mothers on that day really make her feel less than a woman. This is my childhood friend who is bubbling over with quick wit and personality. She does not have self-esteem issues so this revelation startled me. "Less than a woman"... what do you mean? She said she couldn't have children and Mother's Day intensified her pain. The pain of barrenness has touched the lives of women for thousands of years. Hannah is one of several barren women who are recorded in the scriptures. During that time, the culture was brutal if you could not bear a child. The repercussions extended beyond her physical limitations. Hannah was stigmatized. Back then, a woman's value was attached to the number of children she would bore. A childless woman was considered a failure and an embarrassment to her husband. So as it would bear, she was not esteemed socially. To compound her heartache, her husband Ekanah was in his right to divorce her. If that wasn't enough, she endured the constant taunting and insults of her sister-wife Peninnah. Her pain; physical, emotional, and social was at level ten. She had unfulfilled dreams, a rival sister-wife and she was overwhelmed by grief. Sounds like a toxic cocktail for a nervous breakdown. Over the years of serving the women at The Church Without Walls, I have prayed with many women who have faced trials of many kinds: breast cancer, troubled marriages, death of a child, addictions, financial hardships, and spiritual warfare, to name a few. Hypothetically, what if you could select your own trials? How likely is it that you would select something that would cause pain, grief, or any other discomfort? Not likely! Most would not choose anything beyond the magnitude of a chipped nail. It is through our trials that our faith is tested and our walk with God is strengthened.

Read James 1:2. What disposition should you have when facing trials?

_____

_____

It's hard to know the true depth of your character until you see how you react under pressure. According to James 1:3, when your faith is tested what will it develop?

_____

_____

Write James 1:4 then memorize it.

_____

_____

On your walk with God there are lessons to learn in the good times and in hardship. There are several life lessons and spiritual truths we can learn from Hannah's burden, brokenness and blessing:

1. Decide to Do Something About Your Situation v. 9

No one is exempt from trials. The challenge is deciding not to retreat or become a recluse, but to instead move in the direction of help and hope.

Hannah could have continued to complain, and live in agony, distress and misery. But...she made the decision to do something about her situation. Maya Angelou said, "You may not control all the events that happen to you, but you can decide not to be reduced by them."

Hannah reached her breaking point and decided it was time to do something about her craziness! She had endured and suffered for many years. She realized her situation was beyond her control; she needed divine intervention.

Like a woman who has had enough, she stood up from the table and made her way to the church of God.

2. Take Your Cares to God in Prayer v.10

What a Friend We Have in Jesus is one of the timeless hymns of the ages. Its message reminds us that God is a loving Father and friend who is available to carry our burdens and ease our pain.

Slowly read each verse of this hymn. Allow the words to resonate in your heart.

What a friend we have in Jesus, All our sins and griefs to bear! What a privilege to carry Everything to God in prayer! Oh, what peace we often forfeit, Oh, what needless pain we bear, All because we do not carry Everything to God in prayer!

Have we trials and temptations? Is there trouble anywhere? We should never be discouraged—Take it to the Lord in prayer. Can we find a friend so faithful, Who will all our sorrows share? Jesus knows our every weakness; Take it to the Lord in prayer.

Are we weak and heavy-laden, Cumbered with a load of care? Precious Savior, still our refuge—Take it to the Lord in prayer. Do thy friends despise, forsake thee? Take it to the Lord in prayer! In His arms He'll take and shield thee, Thou wilt find a solace there.

Blessed Savior, Thou hast promised Thou wilt all our burdens bear; May we ever, Lord, be bringing All to Thee in earnest prayer. Soon in glory bright, unclouded, There will be no need for prayer—Rapture, praise, and endless worship Will be our sweet portion there.

The children of God have an open invitation to His throne. We can come to Him confidently at any time and unload ALL of our anxieties, worries, physical ailments and spiritual challenges (I Peter 5:7).

3. Appeal to the Sovereignty of God v.11

Elkanah loved his wife, but he could not do anything about her barrenness. Remember, it was God who closed Hannah's womb. She appealed to the God who had the power to open her womb. She said, "O Lord Almighty... (v11)!" God is not only sovereign in principle, but He is also sovereign in practice. All things are under His control. He rules all and nothing happens without His permission or direction. Hannah appealed to El Shaddai, the God of power, strength and might.

R.C. Sproul said, "If there is any element of the universe that is outside of his authority, then he is no longer God over all. In other words, sovereignty belongs to deity. Sovereignty is a natural attribute of the Creator. God owns what he makes, and he rules what he owns." There is no one like the Lord God Almighty. He is superior, supreme in authority and power. His sovereignty has no boundaries or restrictions. According to Psalms 135:6, where does God release His All Mighty power?

_____

_____

4. Pray in Honesty and Humility vv.10-14

Have you ever experienced that sacred intensive prayer time with God? You were completely disconnected from everything around you and it was just you and God. One Sunday, while the congregation was standing for morning prayer, I had a cherished encounter with God. From a place deep within, I wholeheartedly prayed to Him, completely unveiled and broken in His presence. That Sunday morning, I needed Him, I needed Him... I needed Him! I stood with my arms extended toward heaven, tears rolling down my face and my heart calling out to God. He graciously came to my corner seat and took me up to a place where I communed with Him and He with me. It was so beautiful. I understand why the disciples did not want to come down from the mountaintop (Matthew 17:1-9). The young lady seated next to me gently touched me and when I came down from my experience, I realized the congregation had already sat down and I stood alone in my position of surrender. The worship had moved on to the weekly announcements. Imagine how that looked. My prayer was private, though it was offered during corporate worship; it was just God and me, sacred and worshipful.

Hannah prayed from her pain and affliction. In bitterness of soul (v10) Hannah wept much and prayed to the LORD. She mingled her tears with her prayers and was in deep communion with Him. Her lips were moving and no words came from her mouth. Her prayer was intense, honest and pure. There was no façade or mask. It went from her heart directly to God's ears. Eli the priest thought she was drunk. She was not insulted by his accusation. She shared her anguish and he was moved by her sorrow. Read Psalms 34:17-19; 51:17. God is close to the brokenhearted. He is our power, wisdom and courage. It is Him alone who gives us strength to pray when we are burdened and feel like giving up.

5. Be Specific in Your Petition v. 11

God is not absent from our heartache. Hannah asked Him to look on her misery, pain and shame and see the hurt and the tears. She was not general or vague in her request. She was very specific about her heart's desire. She didn't ask God to give her a baby. She asked God for a specific gender, give me a son. Believing that God would answer her prayers, she promised to give the miracle gift of a son back to the Giver. God is our Heavenly Father and He knows our needs and He feels our cares. We have bold access to Him. When our hearts desires are clear, our petition to God will reflect the same.

In Luke 18:35-42 a blind man shamelessly cried out to Jesus for help. Read these passages and notice the exchange between Jesus and the beggar. What did the blind beggar ask of Jesus? (Luke 18:38)

_____

_____

Jesus responded to the beggar's request with a specific question. (Luke 18:41)

_____

_____

The beggar's second request was specific. This time, what did he ask of Jesus? (Luke18:41)

_____

_____

Meditate on 1 John 5:14. *This is the confidence we have in approaching God: that if we ask anything according to his will, he hears us.*

6. Pray Expecting Something to Happen vv.17-18

Your worship in prayer is sacred. It takes you into God's presence and He shows you His will and He prepares you to obey Him. Your prayers are not designed to change God; your prayers are designed to change you. Hannah entered the Temple an emotional wreck.

Look at the following verses and describe her emotions.

vv.7-8 _____

v.10 _____

v.15 _____

v.16 _____

God will use your prayer time to soften your heart and change your focus. After Hannah finished praying, Eli, the priest, encouraged her. A transformation has occurred within Hannah. Her disposition has changed, she has an appetite, her head is lifted and her walk is different. She didn't leave the Temple with a baby, but she left with a renewed strength and the assurance that God would answer her prayer.

How has this lesson challenged your walk with God?

_____

_____

_____

What steps will you take today to go farther in your walk?

Physical Walk _____

_____

Spiritual Walk _____

_____

• •

DAY FOUR
The Woman with the Issue of Blood - Whole Again!

Mark 5:24-35

While Jesus was on His way to heal Jairus' daughter, a nameless woman interrupted him along the way. For twelve years this woman walked through life broken and distraught. Because of her constant bleeding she had no quality of life, she only existed. Every area of her life was shattered, in some unfavorable way. Her infirmity caused her life to spiral into a place of misery. Imagine her load of shame, grief and pain. Put her under a microscope and describe how her infirmity affected her whole life.

Physically

_____

_____

Financially

_____

_____

Emotionally

_____

_____

Socially

_____

_____

Spiritually

_____

_____

Physically

_____

_____

For twelve years her private affliction was a public matter. According to the Leviticus law she was considered unclean. Read Leviticus 15:25-27 and give additional insight on how her illness affected her life.

_____

_____

She looked to doctors for a cure, but they only drained her finances without resolving her ailment.

R.C. Sprouls says, "God uses trials as a megaphone to get our attention." This woman was diseased, desperate and destitute. God had her full attention.

She had lost hope and exhausted all of her options. Her condition prohibited her from engaging in community with others. But, as she hovered in the crowd, she managed to hear what others were saying about Jesus.

- She possibly heard that Jesus healed Peter's mother-in-law and a man with leprosy. (Mark1)

- She could have heard that Jesus healed a paralyzed man. (Mark 2)

- Perhaps she heard that Jesus healed a man with a shriveled hand. (Mark 3)

- I am sure she heard as recorded in Mark 4, how Jesus spoke to the raging sea and told the waters to be still.

- She may have also heard about Jesus healing Legion, the crazy man that live in the cemetery. (Mark 5)

- Perhaps, she overheard Jairus asking Jesus to come and lay hands on his dying daughter. (Mark 5)

She had heard of the miraculous things that Jesus had done for others and it ignited her faith.   She believed, if He could heal and deliver others, surely He could do the same for her. *Faith comes by hearing, and hearing by the word of God* (Romans 10:17).   Her faith swelled up in her and gave her courage and determination. Do you have that bodacious faith that will step over fear?   She took a risk, and quite frankly, what did she have to lose? NOTHING! She had already lost everything. She ignored the crowd. She even ignored the religious order of the day. Have you ever allowed your problems or fears to keep you from God? This obscure woman extended her hand, not to touch Jesus' hand – that would have been too familiar. She extended her hand, not to touch Jesus' head. Never... that gesture would have been irreverent.   She was unclean so she couldn't walk up to Jesus and tell Him publicly about her issue. She had to reach for a private cure.   She didn't say to herself, "If I could just touch Jesus." As she dialogued with herself, what did she say according to (v28)?

_____

_____

She was confident that Jesus' healing power would exude through His clothes so she extended her hand and gave Jesus her broken body.   After she touched Jesus, how long did it take for her bleeding to stop (v29)?

_____

_____

The flow of her disease collided with the healing power of Jesus.   The endless flow of blood that came from her body for 12 years dried up. She regained her strength and felt perfectly well all over her body. Jesus did what doctors could not do.   He is Jehovah Rapha, The LORD our Healer.   He is the healer of all sicknesses, diseases, hurts and disappointments.   That same healing power is unlimited and available to anyone who calls on Him. Do you know God as a healer? Have you ever experienced His healing power? Read Psalm 30:2; 103:1-4. Allow God to speak to you then journal your thoughts or prayers.

_____

_____

For some, physical healing may not take place on earth, but we have the assurance that ultimate healing will take place in heaven. No matter what you are experiencing here on earth, God has written the final chapter of your life.   Read Revelations 21:3-4 and describe what God promises His children.

_____

_____

After she touched his clothes, Jesus asked, "Who touched me?" Why would Jesus ask this question when He knew who touched him? This woman was silent for 12 years. This was her moment, her golden opportunity to open her mouth and confess her healing. Jesus did not want her to go unnoticed for what He had done in her life. How did you respond when God healed you? Were you silent about your blessing?

_____

_____

Why do you think the woman was afraid to confess she was the one who touched Jesus?

_____

_____

She had been powerless and obscure for 12 years. Jesus wanted her to openly confess what He had done to inspire hope and encouragement in others. The great things that God is doing in our lives are not for us to lock in a vault. Someone needs to hear about your healing, deliverance, and freedom. Take time and write your testimony and be prepared to share it when the opportunity permits.

_____

_____

Jesus wanted her to openly confess her healing to bring glory and honor to God. Her healing was not at the hand of her doctors. It was a grace gift from the loving hand of God. No one else can take the credit for her healing. All praise, glory and honor belong to Him!

Jesus was persistent. He wanted a confession. Read v33 and describe how the woman responds to Jesus.

_____

_____

Jesus didn't ask the question to embarrass or condemn the woman. He asked because He wanted to reward her open confession and restore her life. Jesus calls her "daughter," esteeming this once nameless and ostracized woman. The King James Version reads, "Daughter, thy faith hath made thee whole; go in peace, and be whole of thy plague." He healed her of the dreadful excessive bleeding and put her fragmented life back together. Yes, He restored her, making her completely whole again!

He restored her _____ – she was healed from the excessive flow of blood. She was cleansed and strengthened.

He restored her _____ – she was no longer destitute. Her heavenly Father is rich and He owns the cattle of a thousand hills.

He restored her _____ – she is no longer stigmatized as the woman with the issue of blood, or the unclean woman. Jesus esteemed her and gave her worth by publicly calling her "Daughter."

He restored her _____ – she is no longer ostracized. She can return to family gatherings, the market place, but most of all she can return to the Temple of God.

He restored her _____ – now she has joy, peace, contentment, hope, courage, but most of all she has faith!

It takes faith to begin the process of restoration. This woman had a great need and she had the faith to reach out to Jesus for her healing. You should never allow your fear to keep you from approaching Jesus. You can come to Him in faith. He will honor your faith, restore the broken pieces of your life, and give you a new beginning. It is impossible to walk confidently with God without faith.

How has this lesson challenged your walk with God?

_____

_____

What steps will you take today to go farther in your walk?

Physical Walk   _____

_____

Spiritual Walk   _____

_____

DAY FIVE
Walking with a Legend

*Select a woman who has influenced your life or
select a woman in the Bible that was not discussed in this week's lesson.
Complete the following:*

The supporting Scripture(s):

Her name:

Her husband:

The meaning of her name:

Her character:

Her challenges:

Her great accomplishments:

Her failure(s):

What are your similarities?

How has this special woman influenced your life?

The best stories aren't about people with a nice past. They are about people who SURVIVED a bad past, lived their dream and had a happy ending.

Sonya Parker

WEEK FOUR

Walking in Victory

Matthew 6:25-34

A few summers ago while on vacation, I would rise early and enjoy lovely morning walks along the island coastline. Well, this particular morning I decided to listen to my gospel music. Walter Hawkins and Daryl Coley were playing through my iPod and a gentle sea breeze would occasionally hit my face. It was a glorious walk, reflective and meditative. As I listened to Daryl Coley's song, "God and God Alone" and beheld the tropical view, I extended my hands toward heaven and worshipped as I walked. While in my zone of worship and praise, I anticipated the next Daryl Coley song. Much to my surprise, some rapper person starts singing, "*You know you like that.*" I stopped abruptly and I advanced to the next song and it was "Int'l Players Anthem." I didn't put this music on my iPod. What happened to my praise music? Who is UGK (Underground Kingz)? I pulled the headset from my ears and knew my son was to blame. Why would he sync his iPod with MY computer? I don't want a rap album in my music library. Needless to say, my worshipful meditative walk had changed to an angry woman's trot. I went from a spirit of praise to being livid!

You are on a victory walk with God. However, you will encounter potholes or unleveled ground along the path. Worry, anger, and fear are the snares that will make your walk an obstacle course. The challenge is not to succumb to anything that will consume your thought life and shake your faith. Instead, recognize each snare as an opportunity to walk closely with God, trusting in His power and growing in His word.

While walking with God this week you will learn:

- Worrying is a sin and it displeases God.
- God's love is the antidote for fear.
- Out of control anger will hinder your spiritual growth.
- How to forgive through Magic Eyes.
- To pause, reflect and pray.

Song of Meditation: *I Will Trust In The Lord*

DAY ONE
Worrying...A Waste of Time
Matthew 6:25-34

Glenn Turner says, "Worrying is like a rocking chair, it gives you something to do, but it gets you nowhere." In Jesus' Sermon on the Mount of Olives, he leaned in heavy on the matter of worry. Out of nine verses, 25-34, he mentions the word "worry" six times. He warns us against allowing worry to consume our thoughts and rob us of precious time, valuable time that should be assigned to productive and meaningful things. We often allow the insignificant to take precedence over the significant. Life is more than all the clothes, money and land you can acquire. Those are just material things and Jesus reminds us that our lives are far more important–He wants us to trust in Him to supply our needs. He is the giver of life and He can be trusted with all the details of our life.

List the things that cause you to worry.

_____

_____

Write verse 25. Underline the things Jesus asked us not to worry about.

_____

_____

After my iPod debacle, I felt the best way for me to regroup was to enjoy the breakfast buffet. As I sat at my table waiting for my husband to join me, I noticed how the birds waited patiently for people to step away from their tables so they could feast on the unattended plates. These sparrows would help themselves to whatever pieces of food that remained. And yes, they dined well. Even though they did not make a reservation, wait to be seated, order from a menu, or pay for their meal they received their daily nourishment at the expense of someone else. At that moment, verse 26 became clear to me. Those little birds were not worried about what they were going to eat the next day. They ate to sustain their strength for that day. So often we worry ourselves into a medical crisis by taking on the cares of tomorrow. Worrying about the future robs us of our present. It is impossible to accomplish or fulfill the obligations of today when you are consumed with the worries of tomorrow. Tomorrow, however, is not promised to us, nor does it belong to us. When we live in today, the present, it keeps us from being consumed with the cares of tomorrow.

Write Matthew 6:11.

_____

_____

It is selfish and quite arrogant to believe that we are capable of sustaining and providing for ourselves. Our Heavenly Father holds all tomorrows. When we ask God to take care of the needs for today, we are acknowledging that He is the provider of all things and we must rely on His power and graciousness to sustain us.

There is NO benefit in worrying. NONE! Yet, we allow this useless time zapper to take us away from the significant things and off the righteous path. It is important to realize that worrying is a tool of the enemy. He wants us to worry because it is a distraction that lures us from a life of prayer, faith and trust. It is the Word of God that gives us the courage and the ability to walk in victory with Him. Search the following passages. Write God's prescription for living victoriously over worrying.

1. Philippians 4:6-7, I Peter 5:7

_____

_____

2. Psalm 1:1-2, Isaiah 26:3

_____

_____

3. II Corinthians 12:7-10

_____

_____

4. II Corinthians 1:20

_____

_____

5. Isaiah 40:29-31

_____

_____

6. Matthew 6:33-34

_____

_____

Worry is an uninvited guest. You can rest assured that there will always be a line of worries knocking at the front door of your mind. As soon as one worry exits, there is another one waiting to enter. You can experience victory over your worries. Prayer is your greatest weapon. Meditating on God's Word will keep your mind in perfect peace (Isaiah 26:3).

In Philippians 4:8, Paul gives a list of virtues we should think about to keep our minds spiritually focused. Write each virtue below.

_____

_____

Like Paul, your life may be pierced with a thorn (II Corinthians 12:7). It is not wise to worry about what you cannot change; instead rest in God's sustaining grace. There are over 7,000 promises in the Bible. Recite His promises to gain strength and sing songs of praise to release your joy. Worrying is a lack of faith and trust in God. Wait on Him to fulfill His promise. Seek the Kingdom of God above all else, and live righteously, and He will give you everything you need.

How has this lesson challenged your walk with God?

_____

_____

_____

What steps will you take today to go farther in your walk?

Physical Walk _____

_____

Spiritual Walk _____

_____

· ·

DAY TWO
Power... Not Fear!

II Timothy 1:3-8

One of the most notable men in scripture, the Apostle Paul, writes from a Roman prison a letter of encouragement and instruction to his protégé and co-laborer in the faith, young Timothy. While looking at death by execution, Paul writes this letter out of his love for the church and the Christian faith. In his letter, he passes on to Timothy the torch of leadership and lovingly instructs him as a father would his own son. Paul's genuine concern and love for his young friend is evident in his writing. He reminded him that he grew up in the presence of strong women of faith and that faith now lives in him and he is recognized as a respected man of faith. Paul also reminded Timothy that he had everything that he needed to continue the ministry work. Paul knew that Timothy was facing opposition because of his leadership and young age. He felt this caused him to become apprehensive or fearful about fulfilling his calling. God does not ask us to fear people.

Although, people can be intimidating, servants of God must stand firm and not succumb to this kind of pressure. Fearing people will cause you to become ineffective in your work for God. *Fear of man will prove to be a snare, but whoever trusts in the Lord is kept safe* (Proverbs 29:25).

Do you fear people more than you fear God?

_____

_____

What assignment has God given to you and you have allowed fear to hold you hostage?

_____

_____

Why are you afraid to trust God and move forward in faith?

_____

_____

Fear has stifled many dreams, opportunities, goals and aspirations. These dreams are still on the shelf or stuffed in a shoebox in a closet waiting to be fulfilled. Paul encouraged Timothy to be bold and step out on faith. He was ordained to do ministry work and Paul did not want fear to paralyze him from fulfilling his obligations. On the other hand, Timothy knew firsthand about the persecution and trials that Paul faced during his ministry. He also knew that there was a strong possibility that he might face the same fate as his mentor. The thought of the mistreatment and oppression Paul endured had the young man shaking in his boots. That's what fear does; it takes the unknown and magnifies it into a distorted reality. The insightful acronym for fear—False Evidence Appearing Real—helps to put this notion in perspective. We need a sound mind to see things from God's perspective. God gave us the Holy Spirit to walk alongside of us, to plant truth in our mind and remind us of God's will (John 14:26).

Fear is destructive and when you live under the weight of it the outcome is disobedience and second-guessing what God has clearly assigned for your life. After my youngest son completed his undergraduate studies, he shared with me that the Lord was leading him to attend seminary. Knowing his temperament,

I thought to myself, wow, I didn't see that one coming. I trusted his obedience to follow where God was leading him. After his first semester of intense papers, presentations, fieldwork, and reports, he began to question whether he clearly heard what God had assigned him to do. Fear will cause you to doubt God when you face challenges, trials and persecution. This is not the time to give in to fear or doubt your God-ordained assignment. This is the time to trust God wholeheartedly and walk in confidence with Him! Let's be real...it is the enemy's tactic to scare you out of doing anything that will bring glory and honor to God. The enemy wants your fears to hold you hostage. The devil is a LIAR! Fear is not from God. He gave us three beautifully wrapped gifts that will extinguish fear from our lives: love, power and a sound mind (II Timothy 1:7). Our human spirit is empowered by God's Holy Sprit and this power propels us and makes us conquerors...more than conquerors through Jesus Christ (Romans 8:37).

The servant leader, Joshua, gives a vivid picture of how the children of God should respond when God gives us an assignment. After the death of Moses, Joshua was appointed by God to assume the responsibility as Israel's new leader. Every new job is frightening and a challenge without the presence of God. When God is with you and you rely on His power fear has to flee. Read Joshua 1 and notice how Joshua takes the mantle without any trepidation.

Look at Joshua 1:6, 7, and 9. When God commissioned Joshua, how many times did He tell him to "be strong and courageous"?

_____

_____

According to Joshua 1:16-18 how did the people continue to encourage Joshua?

_____

_____

After reading Joshua's story, what is God saying to you regarding your fear(s)?

_____

_____

Joshua's new job consisted of leading over two million people into a new land that they had to conquer first...and they DID IT! Likewise, Paul encouraged Timothy to boldly exercise his ministry gifts without fear or shame.

God's love will silence your fears and give you the faith to walk in confidence with Him. His love is the antidote that will drive away all fears. The following passages will remind you of His love and power. Search the scriptures and fill in the blank.

1. *Exodus 20:20* - Moses said to the people, "Do not be _____. God has come to test you, so that the _____ of God will be with you to keep you from sinning."

2. *Proverbs 1:7* - The _____ of the Lord is the beginning of knowledge, but fools despise wisdom and instruction.

3. *Philippians 4:13* - I can do all this through _____ who gives me _____.

4. *I John 4:18* - There is no _____ in love. But perfect love drives out _____, because _____ has to do with punishment. The one who _____ is not made perfect in love.

How has this lesson challenged your walk with God?

_____

_____

_____

What steps will you take today to go farther in your walk?

Physical Walk   _____

_____

Spiritual Walk   _____

_____

. . . .

DAY THREE
Getting It Under Control!
Ephesians 4:26

One summer at my home church, the youth choir hosted various events to raise money to offset the cost of our new choir robes. We washed cars and offered concessions, baked goods and beverages. In the Texas heat, we worked hard and did everything within legal boundaries to raise money. There were two young ladies in the choir who found our method of fundraising a little beneath the standards of their well-manicured hands. They did not wash a car, sell a teacake or put mustard on a hot dog. They contributed no visible or moral support to our cause. The day came for us to order the robes and guess who were the first two in line? You got it! As the president of the choir, I thought it was my responsibility to voice my complaint to the pastor. I went to his office and shared my concern and concluded my well-crafted speech with, " because they did not help raise the money they will not be getting robes." I knew he was going to agree with me. Instead, his reply was, "Yes, the church will purchase their robes as well." I restated my complaint and again he firmly replied, "They are members of the youth choir and they are also getting robes." Well, I am ebony-hued, kissed heavily by the sun, and right before his eyes, I turned BEET RED! My eyes began to well up with tears and I lost it. Why should they get robes? They thought they were too good to help with the fundraising. We worked hard and they did nothing!! That's not FAIR! I was so angry. I left his office and cried all the way home. The first Sunday that we sang in our new robes was supposed to be a joyous day. When I saw those two in their robes... I became angry all over again! I thought to myself, instead of those beautiful white and burgundy robes, they should have on t-shirts with the word "SLACKERS" across the front... in large arial black font. My Sunday morning choir robe anger stewed for weeks until one Sunday the Lord let me know that I could not minister in truth to His people with so much anger in my heart. My anger was affecting my worship and my praise offering. I had to get it under control because it was getting the better of me.

In lesson two we saw the wrath of God. He destroyed the city of Sodom and Gomorrah because the people were blatantly disobedient. In Mark 3:1-6, Jesus openly expressed His anger with the Pharisees because of their callous attitude toward others. There is nothing wrong with anger. What you do with it and the way you express it is the concern. Jesus expressed His anger without sinning. He instead flipped a negative into a positive. He used His anger as a constructive solution and healed a man's hand. Anger is not wrong when it is directed at sin or the mistreatment of others.

Read I Samuel 11:1-7. Saul was angered by the Ammonites' mistreatment of the Israelites. Do you feel his anger was justified?

_____

_____

How do you respond when you feel others are being mistreated?

_____

_____

According to v6, Saul burned with anger. Can you identify with this type of anger? If so, how did you respond? Did you throw a hairbrush, use profanity, slam the door...? Or did you take a more positive approach?

_____

_____

Anger is a powerful emotion; it can certainly be explosive. The Holy Spirit used Saul's anger to make a difference. He directed that energy to bring freedom and justice to the Israelites. When you are angered by some sin or injustice that is not the time to lose it. Ask God to give you power to channel your anger in positive ways; so that, it can make a change for the better.

We have permission to be angry, but that anger must operate within the boundaries of self-control (Ephesians 4:26). Do you exercise self-control when you are angry?

_____

_____

Read Proverbs 16:32 and fill in the blank.
Better a patient person than a warrior, one with _____ than one who takes a city.

Self-control is a fruit of the Spirit (Galatians 5:23). Out of control anger is a sin. It will lead you to act in a way that is destructive to your Christian walk. When God rejected Cain's offering and accepted Abel's offering Cain did the unthinkable. Cain invited his brother to join him in the field and out of his jealous anger he killed him. God saw the crime scene and put Cain under a curse. It was Cain and not Abel who did wrong. His anger was out of control and it led him to commit murder (Genesis 4:2-8).

Read Proverbs 25:28. How did the Proverbs writer describe a man who lacks self- control?

_____

_____

An out of control life is like a city without the protection of the great walls. You are exposed and open to all sorts of attacks from the enemy.

Has anger ever pushed you to a point where you said something or did something that took you completely out of your character or out of the will of God?

_____

_____

Anger will keep you from developing and growing spiritually. Each day you should strive to please God in your walk with Him. Yes, to strive is to use self-control and not be compelled to give someone a piece of your mind. Keep that peace and use it to honor God.

My son left a can of soda in the freezer overnight and the next day it exploded and sprayed everything in the freezer. That is the image of unharnessed anger. It is out of control and lashes out at blameless people and innocent bystanders. This type of behavior reveals a much deeper problem. It is selfish anger and no one benefits from it.

Look at Numbers 22:21-30. Give your assessment of Balaam's actions.

_____

_____

Have you ever taken your anger out on someone who didn't deserve it?

_____

_____

When someone or something begins to ignite the flame of anger, before you turn up the heat, look for the cause. A quick-tempered man does foolish things (Proverb 14:17). Balaam was so blinded by his anger he couldn't see what was right in front of him. He was ready to kill his loyal donkey for acting out of character. The donkey saw what Balaam was unable to see and her awkward response is what saved Balaam's life.

Do you see yourself as a person who easily angers? Do your friends or family refer to you as "Angry Bird"? Sometime there is truth attached to negative accusations. It is worth pausing and taking some time to reflect on your anger gauge.

_____

_____

Make a list of the things that make you angry.

_____

_____

Do you resolve your anger matters within 24 hours or do you stew over them? (Ephesians 4:26)

_____

_____

The New Testament writers recorded occasions when Jesus was angry and tempted, much like us, but He did not sin (Hebrews 4:15). The practice of getting anger under control begins with what is in your heart and what comes from your mouth. Search the following scriptures and match the correct corresponding answer.

1. _____ Proverbs 15:1   A. Do not make friends with a hot-tempered person.

2. _____ Proverbs 15:28   B. Whoever conceals their sins does not prosper.

3. _____ Proverbs 22:24-25   C. Fools give full vent to their rage.

4. _____ Proverbs 28:13   D. Everyone should be quick to listen, slow to speak.

5. _____ Proverbs 29:11   E. A gentle answer turns away wrath.

6. _____ James 1:19   F. The heart of the righteous weighs its answer.

Correct Answers:1.E 2.F 3.A 4.B 5.C 6.D

How has this lesson challenged your walk with God?

_____

_____

_____

What steps will you take today to go farther in your walk?

Physical Walk   _____

_____

Spiritual Walk   _____

_____

• •

DAY FOUR
How Many Times...?
Matthew 18:21-35

One lovely afternoon, my dear friend and I were having lunch and she shared with me that it is not a challenge for her to extend forgiveness to someone who has hurt her. She said, when she forgives, she is done and she moves on. Now that's spiritual maturity! Well, I'm not quite there yet. Some people can forgive in a flash, while for others, forgiveness is a process and may take a little more time. *The Magic Eyes* is a fable that gives the spiritual, emotional, and physical effects of holding on to unforgiveness. It also gives the illustration of freedom and life when the burden of unforgiveness is lifted. Read the short tale and open your heart to receive the liberating message of forgiveness.

The Magic Eyes: A Little Fable
Excerpt from Lewis Smedes, Forgive and Forget: Healing the Hurts We Don't Deserve

In the village of Faken in innermost Friesland there lived a long thin baker named Fouke, a righteous man, with a long thin chin and a long thin nose. Fouke was so upright that he seemed to spray righteousness from his thin lips over everyone who came near him; so the people of Faken preferred to stay away.

Fouke's wife, Hilda, was short and round, her arms were round, her bosom was round, her rump was round. Hilda did not keep people at bay with righteousness; her soft roundness seemed to invite them instead to come close to her in order to share the warm cheer of her open heart. Hilda respected her righteous husband, and loved him too, as much as he allowed her; but her heart ached for something more from him than his worthy righteousness. And there, in the bed of her need, lay the seed of sadness.

One morning, having worked since dawn to knead his dough for the ovens, Fouke came home and found a stranger in his bedroom lying on Hilda's round bosom. Hilda's adultery soon became the talk of the tavern and the scandal of the Faken congregation. Everyone assumed that Fouke would cast Hilda out of his house, so righteous was he. But he surprised everyone by keeping Hilda as his wife, saying he forgave her as the Good Book said he should.

In his heart of hearts, however, Fouke could not forgive Hilda for bringing shame to his name. Whenever he thought about her, his feelings toward her were angry and hard; he despised her as if she were a common whore. When it came right down to it, he hated her for betraying him after he had been so good and so faithful a husband to her. He only pretended to forgive Hilda so that he could punish her with his righteous mercy. But Fouke's fakery did not sit well in heaven.

So each time that Fouke would feel his secret hate toward Hilda, an angel came to him and dropped a small pebble, hardly the size of a shirt button, into Fouke's heart. Each time a pebble dropped, Fouke would feel a stab of pain like the pain he felt the moment he came on Hilda feeding her hungry heart from a stranger's larder.

Thus he hated her the more; his hate brought him pain and his pain made him hate. The pebbles multiplied. And Fouke's heart grew very heavy with the weight of them, so heavy that the top half of his body bent forward so far that he had to strain his neck upward in order to see straight ahead. Weary with hurt, Fouke began to wish he were dead.

The angel who dropped the pebbles into his heart came to Fouke one night and told him how he could be healed of his hurt. There was one remedy, he said, only one, for the hurt of a wounded heart. Fouke would need the miracle of the magic eyes. He would need eyes that could look back to the beginning of his hurt and see his Hilda, not as a wife who betrayed him, but as a weak woman who needed him. Only a new way of looking at things through the magic eyes could heal the hurt flowing from the wounds of yesterday.

Fouke protested. "Nothing can change the past," he said. "Hilda is guilty, a fact that not even an angel can change." "Yes, poor hurting man, you are right," the angel said. "You cannot change the past, you can only heal the hurt that comes to you from the past. And you can heal it only with the vision of the magic eyes." "And how can I get your magic eyes?" pouted Fouke.

"Only ask, desiring as you ask, and they will be given you. And each time you see Hilda through your new eyes, one pebble will be lifted from your aching heart." Fouke could not ask at once, for he had grown to love his hatred. But the pain of his heart finally drove him to want and to ask for the magic eyes that the angel had promised. So he asked. And the angel gave.

Soon Hilda began to change in front of Fouke's eyes, wonderfully and mysteriously. He began to see her as a needy woman who loved him instead of a wicked woman who betrayed him.

The angel kept his promise; he lifted the pebbles from Fouke's heart, one by one, though it took a long time to take them all away. Fouke gradually felt his heart grow lighter; he began to walk straight again, and somehow his nose and his chin seemed less thin and sharp than before. He invited Hilda to come into his heart again, and she came, and together they began again a journey into their second season of humble joy.

The Magic Eyes shows how the weight of unforgiveness will affect your whole life. List the devastating effects of holding on to unforgiveness.

Spiritually _____

_____

Physically _____

_____

Emotionally _____

_____

Other _____

_____

Forgiveness is not about the other person it is about you. In forgiveness, your healing, spiritual, physical, and emotional health is at the center, and not the offense or the offender. Smedes said, "The hurt that creates a crisis of forgiving has three dimensions. It is always *personal, unfair, and deep*. When you feel this kind of three dimensional pain, you have a wound that can be healed only by forgiving the one who wounded you." During my walk with God, I have received the grace gift of God's forgiveness for all my sins. I have learned that it is my responsibility as a believer to extend forgiveness to others. It is not a matter for discussion; it is a matter of obedience to His Word (Colossians 3:13). As I surrendered my will to Him, He began to work on my heart in the process (Philippians 1:6).

In Matthew 18:21-35, Jesus taught the meaning of forgiveness. In His ministry, He also demonstrated

His willingness to forgive those who needed it.

Search the following passages. Write the corresponding person who Jesus willingly forgave.

Matthew 9:2-8   _____

Luke 7:44-50   _____

Luke 23:34   _____

Luke 23:39-43   _____

John 18:15-18,
25-27; 21:15-19   _____

In addition to learning the significance of forgiving others, in Matthew 18:21-35, Jesus also teaches that we should not keep a record of how many times we have forgiven someone. Imagine if Jesus kept a file of all the times He has forgiven us. He puts no limit on His love, generosity or grace. Forgiveness is neither a one-time occurrence nor a one person choice. How many times should we forgive? Peter said seven times which is the number of completion. Jesus answered, seventy times seven, signifying to always forgive. He continued to forgive even while He was dying on the cross (Luke 23:39-43). How many times should we forgive? Well, forgiveness for some may be a life long journey. We must continue to forgive until our hearts are completely set free from anger, hurt, resentment and bitterness.   This relief comes through fervent prayer.

After a long flight, I decided to begin my summer vacation with an aromatherapy massage. The masseuse introduced herself and went on to say that she believes massage therapy is a form of healing. She said if I had any unforgiveness in my heart I would not enjoy the massage. OK... before she began, she kindly asks me to pray to "my" God and she would pray to "hers". She then turned to the wall and began to hum and chant. Yes, that's what I said...hum and chant! Well, my forgiveness column was clear...or so I thought. I complied and I turned inwardly and began to pray, asking God to remove any unforgiveness I was harboring in my heart (Psalms 139:23-24). As she started to massage my back she said, you have more lumps and knots in your back than I have in my driveway. Why are you carrying this load? Did those who caused these knots pay to come with you on YOUR vacation? While she worked on my back, God was working on my heart. As I drifted to sleep, He showed me vividly the person that I had not forgiven. I thought I had, but not completely. In that moment I surrendered to God and I asked Him to remove any residue of animosity, set my heart free of unforgiveness, and ease the hurt from my memory. God answered my prayer and...THAT WAS THE BEST MASSAGE...**EVER!!!**

Read Matthew 6:14-15 and complete the following:

For if you forgive men when they sin against you, _____

_____

But if you do not forgive men their sins, _____

_____

According to Mark 11:25 why is it important to forgive others?

_____

_____

Write Ephesians 4:32.

_____

_____

How has this lesson challenged your walk with God?

_____

_____

_____

What steps will you take today to go farther in your walk?

Physical Walk _____

_____

Spiritual Walk _____

_____

• •

DAY FIVE
Going Farther

Today, you are encouraged to revisit each lesson that you studied this week. Take the opportunity to finish the portions of the lesson you were unable to complete. Write questions from each lesson that will enhance a meaningful dialogue with your group or friends.

DAY ONE - *Worry...A Waste Of Time*
Matthew 6:25-34

Write discussion questions from this lesson.

_____

_____

_____

_____

"Worrying is carrying tomorrow's load with today's strength- carrying two days at once. It is moving into tomorrow ahead of time. Worrying doesn't empty tomorrow of its sorrow, it empties today of its strength."
- Corrie ten Boom

Going Farther
How far will you go with God today? He is calling you to go deeper in your walk with Him. When you commit to going farther with God, the sacrifice does not compare to the sacred moments you will experience along the way. Read Psalm 37:3-5 and I Peter 5:7. Ask God to forgive you for wasting precious time worrying instead of trusting Him. Journal your prayer.

DAY TWO - *Power...Not Fear!*
II Timothy 1:3-8

Write discussion questions from this lesson.

_____

_____

_____

_____

"You block your dream when you allow your fear to become bigger than your faith." –Mary Manin Morrissey

Going Farther
How far will you go with God today? He is calling you to go deeper in your walk with Him. When you commit to going farther with God, the sacrifice does not compare to the sacred moments you will experience along the way. Read Mark 6:45-50. Ask God to allow His calming presence to quiet your fears and give you peace. Journal your prayer.

DAY THREE - *Getting It Under Control*
Ephesians 4:26

Write discussion questions from this lesson.

_____

_____

_____

_____

"For every minute you remain angry, you give up sixty seconds of peace of mind." -Ralph Waldo Emerson

Going Farther
How far will you go with God today? He is calling you to go deeper in your walk with Him. When you commit to going farther with God, the sacrifice does not compare to the sacred moments you will experience along the way. Read Matthew 5:22-24. Have you harmed someone or fractured a relationship because of your anger? Ask God to clear the path then go to your brother or sister in the spirit of love and reconciliation. Journal your prayer.

DAY FOUR - *How Many Times...?*
Matthew 18:21-35

Write discussion questions from this lesson.

_____

_____

_____

_____

Lewis B. Smedes wrote in his book, *Forgive and Forget*, "*When you release the wrongdoer from the wrong, you cut a malignant tumor out of your inner life. You set a prisoner free, but you discover that the real prisoner was yourself.*"

Going Farther
How far will you go with God today? He is calling you to go deeper in your walk with Him. When you commit to going farther with God, the sacrifice does not compare to the sacred moments you will experience along the way. Write the name of the person who hurt you. With a sincere heart, ask God to bless that person with His rich abundant blessings. Journal your prayer.

No, in all these things we are more than conquerors through him who loved us.

Romans 8:37

WEEK FIVE

Faithful in Prayer

Spending time in prayer is essential for the life of the believer. During one of my private prayer retreats, I went before God with a list of my frustrations. I had a well-crafted list of complaints about my husband, children and my life. I fervently prayed to God and unloaded on Him every care and heart concern. I wanted God to come in and turn things upside down. That's right, get them God, they are making me tired! As I cried and complained the Holy Spirit ushered me into God's presence and to my surprise showed me..."ME!" What? I went to God with one agenda and He redirected my prayers and showed me His will for my life. My complaints became intercessions for my husband/pastor, my sons, their future, their walk with God, my sons' academic journeys and their future as fathers, husbands and so on. None of those things were on my "I'm going to tell God on you" list. Has that ever happened to you? God had something that He wanted me to do. I needed to get to a quiet place where I could hear from Him. It was my frustrations that led me to His throne. As I communed with Him and He revealed His will I began to see my list of complaints as petty and trivial.

While walking with God this week you will learn:
- God will reveal His will during your time of prayer.
- Prayer is hard work that requires intense labor.
- God looks for our thankfulness.
- The necessity of praying for yourself.
- Going the distance in prayer.

Song of Meditation: *I Found the Answer*

· ·

DAY ONE

Your Prayer...His Will

Exodus 32

Moses took residency on Mount Sinai and communed with God for about forty days. It was there that God gave this servant leader His law inscribed in stones along with other directives for His people. The children of Israel lived in captivity for about 400 years. They are now free from the oppressive hand of Pharaoh. Egypt is behind them and the bright hope of the Promised Land is before them. Before they could move forward, there were matters that God wanted to address with his leader. While Moses was on the mountain receiving the law from God, the people became impatient and weary from waiting for his return. They were in captivity for 400 years but couldn't wait 40 days for Moses to return...imagine that. This was a perfect opportunity for them to trust in the God who delivered them and pray for their leader, Moses. Instead, they approached Aaron and stated, "Make us gods who will go before us. As for this fellow Moses who brought us up out of Egypt, we don't know what has happened to him" (v1). Aaron complied and built a golden calf for them to worship. He completely disregarded the covenant they made a few days earlier. They sinned greatly.

Read Exodus 19:5-8. Write the covenant that the Israelites agreed to obey.

_____

_____

Read Exodus 20:22-23. What did God command Moses to tell them?

_____

_____

Moses' 40 days with God took a drastic shift when God informed him of the corruptions that were going on at the base of the mountain. Moses was not aware of their desperate condition. They forgot God's mighty work and their holy covenant. God was not pleased and threatened to destroy all the people (v10). As God revealed to Moses all that was at stake, he was overtaken with compassion for the people. Read Moses' prayers of intercession for his people Exodus 32:11-14, 30-35.

God had formed Moses into a mighty intercessor. His prayers of intercession were sacrificial and loving. When you are quiet before God, He will use your prayer time to soften your heart and allow you to intercede for others.

Read Romans 8:26-27 and allow the Holy Spirit to direct you in praying for someone who has taken the wrong path and lost their way. Journal your prayer and pray fervently!

A Day of Intercession
I urge, then, first of all, that petitions, prayers, intercession and thanksgiving be made for all people
—1 Timothy 2:1

_____

_____

_____

_____
_____
_____
_____
_____
_____
_____
_____
_____
_____
_____
_____
_____
_____
_____
_____
_____
_____
_____
_____
_____
_____

DAY TWO
Don't Stop Praying!

Luke 18:1-8

Are you persistent in prayer? Do you give up easily when you don't receive an immediate answer? In this parable of the widow and the unjust judge, Jesus is teaching His disciples the importance of being persistent in prayer. The judge was not only unjust, he was also an ungodly man. He had no regard for God or man. The widow was hoping for a reprieve and repeatedly asked the unjust judge to grant her justice against her adversary. Although he rejected her request many times, she did not become weary or discouraged. She was persistent! She asked again...and again...and again believing she would get an answer. Because she did not give up, the unjust judge gave in (v5). If the unjust judge reluctantly answered the widow's request how much more will a loving father do for his children? God is just! He is our Heavenly Father and He is on our side when we pray. His Holy Spirit helps us when we pray. He interprets our groans when we don't know what to pray (Romans 8:26). God loves us and He wants to answer our prayers and give us our heart's desires (Psalm 37:4).

Prayer is work and, like the widow, we should remain persistent and encouraged in the labor. When our prayers are not answered immediately, it is for our good. Our persistence in prayer is transforming. It strengthens our faith, tests our patience and builds our character into the likeness of Christ. Laboring keeps us in constant contact with God and draws us closer to Him. According to II Corinthians 12:1-9, Paul was afflicted by a debilitating physical problem. Whatever this thorn was, it became a hindrance to his ministry and life work. He prayed that God would remove the thorn from his flesh. God did not remove it, but gave Paul what he needed to sustain him along the way. Have you become weary and stopped praying over a life matter or circumstance? God is not like the unjust judge, so don't stop praying! Read I Thessalonians 5:17 and James 5:16b. Go to the throne of God AGAIN. Pray about that concern not in unbelief, but in a refreshed spirit of faith, hope and trust. Journal your prayer.

Pray Continually!
The prayer of a righteous person is powerful and effective. James 5:16b

---

_____

_____

_____

_____

_____

_____

_____

_____

_____

_____

_____

* *

DAY THREE

Thank You!

Luke 17:15-16

The ten lepers encountered Jesus and desperately called out for Him to heal them. He told them to show themselves to the priests. As they obeyed, they were healed (v14). When one of them saw he was healed, he went back to Jesus, praising God in a loud voice; thanking Him and worshipping Him. Jesus asked, "Were not all ten cleansed, where are the other nine?" We have so much to thank God for and God looks for our thankfulness. Beyond the superficial—cars, houses, jewelry, and other material possessions—He lavishes us with love, forgiveness and grace. That is reason enough to say, "Thank you!"

List five areas of your life that you are most grateful:

1. _____

2. _____

3. _____

4. _____

5. _____

Like the nine, it is so easy to get caught up in the blessings that we completely forget the source. Our worship, prayers, service, and daily life should be saturated with gratefulness to God. When I pause and reflect on the great things God has done in my life, my family and my church, like the one that returned, my soul rejoices and cries out to the Grace Giver...THANK YOU!

If you are feeling burdened by your health, finances, family or some other challenging circumstance, pause and give thanks to the God who is bigger than anything you are facing and watch your cares become a grain of sand in the ocean of His grace.

Read Psalm 107:1-3: "Oh, thank God—he's so good! His love never runs out. All of you set free by God, tell the world! Tell how he freed you from oppression, Then rounded you up from all over the place, from the four winds, from the seven seas" (*The Message*). Think about the many grace gifts God has given to you: salvation, healing, protection and so on. Consider the source of your blessings and journal your prayer of gratitude.

A Prayer of Gratitude

Be joyful always; pray continually; give thanks in all circumstances; for this is God's will for you in Christ Jesus. 1 Thessalonians 5:18

_____

_____

_____

_____

_____

_____

_____

_____

_____

_____

_____

_____

_____

_____

_____

_____

_____

_____

_____

_____

_____

· ·

DAY FOUR
Praying for Yourself

Hebrews 5:7

Do you feel that you can't pray for yourself because you have done something wrong? Do you depend on others to pray for you? When you pray for others, do you also petition God for your own personal needs? Praying for yourself is not a selfish or vain act when your prayers are petitioned in humility. The life of Jesus provides the model for our prayers. Throughout the gospels Jesus offered up many kinds of prayers until the end of His earthly assignment. He was preparing to pay the ultimate price for our sins and He saw the need to pray. His disciple John recorded the different prayers that He prayed in John 17. Look closely at verses 1-5. Jesus began this chapter by first praying for himself. According to these verses, what two things did Jesus ask of his Father?

1. _____

2. _____

You are the person who has the greatest power to advance God's work in your life. You are the person who knows your deepest needs. God is so loving he wants you to cast your cares, hurts, sorrows and pain on Him (I Peter 5:7). Even though God knows your every trial and concern He wants you to call on Him when you face trouble (Psalm 50:15). Throughout the Psalms, David often prayed for himself. He prayed constantly for his own needs and for forgiveness, protection, and direction.

Read David's plea for God's mercy and repentance in Psalm 51.

Memorize verse 10. God wants us to walk in strength and confidence with Him. Meditate on the following scriptures and write the focus of each petition in the blank.

I Chronicles 4:9-10 _____

Matthew 6:10 _____

Ephesians 3:15-19 _____

Colossians 1:9-13 _____

Colossians 4:12 _____

Philippians 1:9-11 _____

Journal a prayer for yourself.

Let Me Pray for Myself!

Ask, and it will be given to you; seek, and you will find; knock, and it will be opened to you. Matthew 7:7

_____

_____

_____

_____

_____

_____

_____

_____

_____

_____

_____

_____

_____

_____

_____

_____

_____

_____

_____

_____

_____

_____

_____

• •

DAY FIVE

Wake Up and Pray!

Matthew 26:36-46

Have you ever been on your knees praying and suddenly drifted off to sleep? Are you so busy that your prayer life has become secondary and as a result you just toss up a few quick prayers? Jesus would often pull away from His ministry obligations and commune with God (Mark 1:35). During those critical times when He was faced with making an important decision He would consult His father in prayer. Search the following scriptures and notice how His life was saturated in prayer. Match the correct scripture with the corresponding answer.

_____ Jesus prayed while it was still dark.	A. Luke 6:12-13
_____ Jesus prayed before selecting His disciples.	B. Mark 1:35-37
_____ Jesus prayed before raising Lazarus from the grave.	C. Luke 23:46
_____ Jesus prayed for strength while dying on the cross.	D. John 11:38-44

Correct Answers: 1. B 2.A 3. D 4. C

How can you walk confidently with God if you don't spend time communing with him? Again, Jesus models the significance of prayer in the life of the believer. Faithfulness in prayer gives us the opportunity to walk closely with God. He reveals Himself and His will to those who are faithful in prayer. There have been times when I sensed the divine pull to rise at three or four in the morning to pray. I must admit on occasion, like the disciples, I gave in to the flesh and chose sleep over prayer (v40). I later regretted missing a sacred opportunity to commune with God. He wanted to talk with me and I rejected His invitation. I chose the comfort of my bed instead of walking in the garden with Him. Jesus invited His disciples to the Garden of Gethsemane to pray with Him during the most critical time of His ministry. He told them He was overwhelmed with sorrow to the point of death (v38). He needed his friends to undergird Him in prayer. They didn't see the urgency of His request and could not go the distance. When they should have been praying, they were all overtaken by sleep. Jesus went the distance. He prayed longer and all alone. Is God calling you to go deeper in your prayer life? Recommit to a fervent life of prayer. Find a quiet place where you can talk to God. Select a time so that you can daily meet with Him. Make whatever sacrifice necessary to remain faithful in prayer. Journal your prayer of commitment.

Going the Distance
Going a little farther, he fell with his face to the ground and prayed. Matthew 26:39

_____

_____

_____

_____

_____

_____

_____

_____

_____

_____

_____

_____

_____

_____

_____

_____

_____

Is prayer your steering wheel or your spare tire?

Corrie ten Boom

WEEK SIX

Pressing On!

Philippians 3:12-14

Not that I have already obtained all this, or have already arrived at my goal, but I press on to take hold of that for which Christ Jesus took hold of me. Brothers and sisters, I do not consider myself yet to have taken hold of it. But one thing I do: Forgetting what is behind and straining toward what is ahead, I press on toward the goal to win the prize for which God has called me heavenward in Christ Jesus.

This week you will revisit highlights from previous lessons. Prepare to dig deeper and grow in the knowledge of God by concentrating on your walk with him. Like Paul, our desire is to experience a fuller and more meaningful life of faith and obedience. This level of spiritual maturity is not surface or base, it is the result of an enduring faith in God and studying God's word. You too can grow towards perfection in Christ if you stay determined and Press On!

While walking with God this week you will learn:

• Participating in gossip is disgraceful and destructive.

• You can trust God to help you make wise choices.

• Life lessons from legends.

• Bitterness affects a person physically and spiritually.

• Taking steps to get rid of bitterness.

Song of Meditation: *Victory is Mine!*

• •

DAY ONE

Week 1 Lesson - Bridle My Tongue

Day One - Just a Little Bit!

Read Proverb 17:28, Ecclesiastes 3:1-8.

Do you like to talk? Do you spend a lot of time on social media? Do you always need to have the last word? There is a time for everything, and a season for every activity under heaven. We can learn from Solomon that there is a time for silence (v7). Can you unplug from people and technology for a time of silence, not merely to rest your vocals, but to clear your mind and hear from God? Consider attending a silent retreat or find a quiet place in your home and unplug. Allow God to speak to you through his Word and prayer. NO TALKING!

Day Three - The Source of the Problem

Miriam was quite outspoken about Moses' leadership style. God was not pleased with her excessive talking and he cursed her with leprosy for seven days. Read 1 Timothy 2:1-2: "I urge, then, first of all, that petitions, prayers, intercession and thanksgiving be made for all people— for kings and all those in authority, that we may live peaceful and quiet lives in all godliness and holiness."

Make a list of those individuals in your life that you look to as persons of authority. Take time to petition God on their behalf with prayers of intercession and thanksgiving.

1. _____
2. _____
3. _____
4. _____
5. _____

Day Four - Spill the Tea!

Do you like to gossip? Do you have friends who like to dish? Gossip is a sin. God is not pleased when we participate in unrighteousness and unwholesome talk. The effect of gossip is disgraceful and destructive, it will destroy a home, church and friendships. Those who gossip are puffed up with pride and pride always precedes a fall (Proverbs 16:18).

Read Proverbs 8:13 and complete the following.

The fear of the Lord is to hate_____; I hate _____ and _____ ,

_____ behavior and _____ speech.

The fear of the Lord corresponds with a contrite heart and a deep reverence towards God that drives us to glorify him in all that we do. The more you fear God and walk in confidence with him, the more you will hate evil.

. . . .

DAY TWO
Week 2 Lesson - An Exit Strategy

Genesis 13
Day One - A Bad Choice!

People make decisions about personal and private matters daily; careers, family concerns, relationships, faith and more. God's children can rely on His wisdom and guidance when we are faced with making important decisions. He knows the way and the path that we should take.

Read Proverbs 2:1-15.

How can one find wisdom?   _____ v.3-6

What does God hold in store for the upright? _____ v.7

What will wisdom save you from?   _____ v.12

God's wisdom is undisclosed to those who are disobedient and foolish.

Relying on your own understanding excludes God from your decisions. Can you trust God's Word to help you make wise choices? It is through our trust and faithfulness to him that he graciously directs our path and helps us make a lifelong series of right choices. Are you currently faced with making a major decision regarding your life? You can get direction through fervent prayer and by meditating on God's Word.

Day Three - Association Brings Assimilation!

Lot's tenure in Sodom was not impactful for the kingdom. He lost his most valuable weapon, his witness. This was the tragic plight of a bright young lady I knew. She was well versed in the scriptures, she loved God and she was a strong witness for him. Like Lot, she became entangled in a life of sin. The deeper she submerged herself into that life; the more it weakened her witness. If salt has no flavor, then it has no value. If there is no distinction between our lives and the world, we are worthless.

Have you become content with ungodliness? Are you a valuable witness or do you hide your light under a bowl? Do you go along with the crowd? Have you allowed sin to dim your light? Read Matthew 5:13-16. Ask God to make you an agent of change in your home, church, community and marketplace.

Day Four – Run For Your Life!

It was hard for Lot to leave the life that he had created in Sodom. It was difficult for him to part with the material possessions, prestige, and power. Lot had succumbed to the evil temptations that Sodom offered. His life had become so entangled; he was probably unaware of any change. That is the craftiness of the enemy. His scheme is to destroy us by focusing on our pride, power, physical needs, and desires. Read Matthew 4:1-11. Jesus was in the desert fasting and praying. Notice how the devil used every trick imaginable to tempt him. Jesus was able to resist every temptation that Satan presented because he knew the scripture and he obeyed it. Temptation is not a sin. The sin is when we give in and disobey God. The devil often tempts us when we are weak and vulnerable, emotionally or physically stressed, tired, or lonely. He has a strategy! Are you living under the weight of a temptation? Have you given in to temptation? Are you entangled in some sin? Like the angels pulled Lot and his family out of the pit of Sodom, there is an exit strategy for you. Read Hebrews 4:14-16.

Did Jesus face temptation?

_____

_____

Did He give in to temptation?

_____

_____

Can He sympathize with you when you are tempted?

_____

_____

How should you approach His throne?

_____

_____

Come to His throne with reverence and a bold assurance and he will meet your needs.

• •

DAY THREE
Week 3 Lesson - Walking with Legends

Day One - Abigail, Until Death Do Us Part

Abigail recognized Nabal's lack of wisdom and poor disposition. In spite of his shortcomings, she remained faithful to him until the day he died. Are you facing challenges in your marriage?

- Pray for the needs of your husband.
- Ask God to strengthen your marriage and increase your faith in him.
- Ask God to shape your marriage according to his Word and use it for His glory.

Are you trusting God for a mate? Are you living an honorable life as a single woman while God is at work? Open your heart to the following prayer opportunities:

- Ask God to grant you his comforting presence, peace and patience.
- Ask God to prepare you as he prepares your future mate.
- Ask God to grant you wisdom to recognize the mate he has prepared for you.

Day Two – Hannah, Burdened...Broken...Blessed!

While in the temple praying from her bitter soul, Hannah made a vow to God. She promised God that, if he would give her a son, she would, in turn, give him back. Hannah followed through on her commitment. She gave Samuel back to God for His service. Have you made commitments and failed to uphold your part? Negligence leaves a bad stain on the heart of the offended. The life lesson from Hannah is to walk in faith and make every effort to honor your commitment. Read Hannah's joyous song of praise – 1Samuel 2:1-10.

Ask God to give you a song of praise!

• •

DAY FOUR
Week 4 Lesson – Walking in Victory

Day Four - How Many Times?

Hebrews 12:15: See to it that no one falls short of the grace of God and that no bitter root grows up to cause trouble and defile many.

Have you noticed that, after you drink a glass of milk, there is still a little residue left in the glass? That residue can be likened to bitterness; it is the residue of anger and unforgiveness. It begins to take root when you allow past hurts to take on a life of their own. Over time, the roots grow deeper and deeper each time you rehearse the offense. My mother has a pecan tree at the edge of her front yard. She didn't plant the tree. The roots from the pecan tree in my grandmother's backyard sprouted up in my mother's front yard. Roots do travel and bitter roots will cross the fence and reach over into other areas of your life and the lives of others as well. Get rid of all bitterness (Ephesians 4:31) because the effect of this root is poisonous and detrimental to the life of the believer. Many health professionals are beginning to see the effects of negative emotions on our physical health. Anger and bitterness have been associated with high blood pressure, cardiovascular disorders, ulcers and other physical ailments.

I have experienced over the years of serving women how bitterness can stain relationships. The Greek word "defile" means to stain or dye. Bitterness is destructive and highly attributed to many fractured friendships, broken homes, separations, and divorces.

Bitterness will also hinder your walk with God. How can you influence others for Christ when your heart is filled with anger, resentment, and unforgiveness?

_____

_____

How can you share your testimony when you are bitter towards your neighbor?

_____

_____

How can you talk of God's love and forgiveness when you have a boulder in your heart?

_____

_____

Saul began his reign as king as a favored and respected ruler. Because of his bitter spirit towards David, his life unfortunately ended in sorrow, defeat and suicide (I Samuel 18-31). After David killed Goliath, Saul's seed of bitterness began to flourish. He became jealous, insecure, angry, suspicious, vengeful and afraid of young David, the one who saved his reputation. Saul's bitterness took complete control of his life. He could not serve God's people with the turmoil he had inside his heart.

How do you feel when you think about those who have hurt or rejected you?

_____

_____

What thought(s) enter your mind?

_____

_____

End this lesson by asking God to help you to **want** to forgive because you know that it is the right thing to do. Tomorrow the journey of uprooting bitterness will begin. Read Luke 6:36-37 and Galatians 2:20 to help you prepare to deal with bitterness. It is Christ who lives in us and who gives us the strength to forgive when we have been deeply hurt. He has never withheld forgiveness from his children. Our faith in God allows him to express that forgiveness through us and toward those who have offended us.

• •

DAY FIVE
Week 4 Lesson - Walking in Victory
Day Four - How Many Times? (Part II)

Hebrews 12:15: See to it that no one falls short of the grace of God and that no bitter root grows up to cause trouble and defile many.

It's time to pull up the bitter roots so that you won't fall short of God's grace. Uprooting is not an easy process, but if you endure, it will be the onset of a new journey toward freedom, obedience and confidence in God. Think about the person(s) who hurt you. In Charles Stanley's book, *Forgiveness*, he gives seven steps you can take to get rid of bitterness. Begin the process below.

1. List the all the ways in which that person offended you.

_____

_____

_____

2. Make a list of your own faults.

_____

_____

_____

3. Make a list of the things you have done for which God has forgiven you.

_____

_____

_____

4. Ask God to help you see your offender as a work in His hands.

_____

_____

_____

5. Ask God to forgive you for your bitterness toward that person.

_____

_____

_____

6. Decide in your heart to take total responsibility for your attitude.

_____

_____

_____

7. If you feel it is appropriate, and will not cause more problems than it solves, go to the person, confess your bitterness, and ask for forgiveness. Remember you are assuming the responsibility for your attitude.

Thank God for healing your heart and giving you the freedom to walk with him in forgiveness and grace.

• •

My Praise Report!

Day Four - How Many Times? (Part II)

Through this study you offered several petitions to God for various matters and concerns. Record your petitions below and as God answers record His responses.

My Petition:

_____

_____

_____

God's Response:

_____

_____

_____

My Petition:

_____

_____

_____

God's Response:

_____

_____

My Petition:

_____

_____

God's Response:

_____

_____

My Petition:

_____

_____

God's Response:

_____

_____

My Petition:

_____

_____

God's Response:

_____

_____

Order my steps in thy Word:
and let not any iniquity have
dominion over me.

Psalm 119:133

Talking to God...

_____

_____

_____

_____

_____

_____

_____

_____

_____

_____

_____

_____

_____

_____

_____

_____

_____

_____

_____

_____

_____

_____

_____

_____

The Lord makes firm the steps of the one who delights in him Psalm 37:23

Talking to God...

_____

_____

_____

_____

_____

_____

_____

_____

_____

_____

_____

_____

_____

_____

_____

_____

_____

_____

_____

_____

_____

_____

_____

_____

_____

_____

...he has preserved our lives and kept our feet from slipping. Psalm 66:9

Talking to God...

_____

_____

_____

_____

_____

_____

_____

_____

_____

_____

_____

_____

_____

_____

_____

_____

_____

_____

_____

_____

_____

_____

_____

Order my steps in thy Word: and let not any iniquity have dominion over me. Psalm 119:133

Talking to God...

The Lord makes firm the steps of the one who delights in him Psalm 37:23

Talking to God...

...he has preserved our lives and kept our feet from slipping. Psalm 66:9

Talking to God...

_____

_____

_____

_____

_____

_____

_____

_____

_____

_____

_____

_____

_____

_____

_____

_____

_____

_____

_____

_____

_____

_____

_____

_____

_____

_____

Order my steps in thy Word: and let not any iniquity have dominion over me. Psalm 119:133

Talking to God...

_____

_____

_____

_____

_____

_____

_____

_____

_____

_____

_____

_____

_____

_____

_____

_____

_____

_____

_____

_____

_____

_____

The Lord makes firm the steps of the one who delights in him Psalm 37:23

Talking to God...

...he has preserved our lives and kept our feet from slipping. Psalm 66:9

Talking to God...

_____

_____

_____

_____

_____

_____

_____

_____

_____

_____

_____

_____

_____

_____

_____

_____

_____

_____

_____

_____

_____

_____

_____

_____

_____

Order my steps in thy Word: and let not any iniquity have dominion over me. Psalm 119:133

Talking to God...

The Lord makes firm the steps of the one who delights in him Psalm 37:23

Talking to God...

...he has preserved our lives and kept our feet from slipping. Psalm 66:9

Talking to God...

Order my steps in thy Word: and let not any iniquity have dominion over me. Psalm 119:133

Talking to God...

_____

_____

_____

_____

_____

_____

_____

_____

_____

_____

_____

_____

_____

_____

_____

_____

_____

_____

_____

_____

_____

_____

_____

_____

The Lord makes firm the steps of the one who delights in him Psalm 37:23

Talking to God...

...he has preserved our lives and kept our feet from slipping. Psalm 66:9

Talking to God...

_____
_____
_____
_____
_____
_____
_____
_____
_____
_____
_____
_____
_____
_____
_____
_____
_____
_____
_____
_____
_____
_____
_____
_____
_____
_____

Order my steps in thy Word: and let not any iniquity have dominion over me. Psalm 119:133

Talking to God...

_____

_____

_____

_____

_____

_____

_____

_____

_____

_____

_____

_____

_____

_____

_____

_____

_____

_____

_____

_____

_____

_____

_____

_____

_____

_____

The Lord makes firm the steps of the one who delights in him Psalm 37:23

Talking to God...

...he has preserved our lives and kept our feet from slipping. Psalm 66:9

Talking to God...

_____
_____
_____
_____
_____
_____
_____
_____
_____
_____
_____
_____
_____
_____
_____
_____
_____
_____
_____
_____
_____
_____
_____

Order my steps in thy Word: and let not any iniquity have dominion over me. Psalm 119:133

About the Author

Sheretta is known for her faith, prayer-life and courage. She exudes confidence in her many roles. She serves as the leader for the Mosaic Women's Ministry. Her fine organizational skills, coupled with her faith, have spawned success in life-changing women's retreats, conferences, empowerment seminars, bible studies, and charitable events. She endeavors to minister to the needs of women from all walks of life. She seeks to equip and encourage women to move beyond mediocrity and live the abundant life that is designed for them.

Sheretta operates within the gifts of teaching, encouragement, administration, and serving.

Sheretta received a Bachelor of Business Administration (B.B.A.) in Computer Information Systems from the University of Houston. She is the mother of two gifts from God, Ralph II and Ralphael. Sheretta is married to Ralph Douglas West, Pastor/Founder of The Church Without Walls in Houston, Texas.